THE
DAILY
LECTIONARY

A weekly guide for
daily bible readings
Advent through Eastertide
Year One

Joseph P. Russell

CONTENTS

The Daily Lectionary
A weekly guide for daily Bible reading
Advent through Eastertide
Year One

A method of daily Bible reading that will add to our appreciation of scripture, and to our experience of worship and daily Christian living is provided by the Episcopal Church's *Book of Common Prayer*, the Anglican Church of Canada's *The Book of Alternative Services* and the *Lutheran Book of Worship.*

In each of these we find a daily lectionary, a listing of passages of scripture for daily reading. The lectionary covers a two-year cycle. After following the full cycle, the reader will have been exposed to all of the books of the New Testament twice and all of the pertinent portions of the Old Testament books once. I say "pertinent" portions of the Old Testament, because the daily lectionary does not include those portions of the Hebrew scripture that are redundant or irrelevant for the Christian.

The Book of Psalms is read in its entirety every seven weeks. Moreover, the biblical texts chosen for reading each day are not picked at random. They follow the ebb and flow of the liturgical church year. Sometimes they reflect the Sunday texts assigned in the Eucharistic lectionary. Thus we read scripture in a way that supports our life as a Christian through the ancient seasons of the church's year. Since the liturgical seasons take us through the fullness of Christian doctrine, we are exposed week in and week out to all aspects of what it means to be alive in Christ. Of all the many methods of Bible reading, this one is tied most closely to what is going on in the rest of the church.

This pattern of Bible reading is ancient. It goes back to our Jewish roots where portions of scripture were (and still are) assigned for study each week. The entire assembly focused on the same texts. Though the texts were often read in the privacy of one's home, they were still read in communion with the rest of the assembly. This is the principle of the daily lectionary as it exists today in the Christian tradition. Some people

1

will read the lectionary with a group of other worshippers. Others will read the scripture alone. But either way, they will read the Bible with the church. We are in communion with each other.

This weekly guide to the daily lectionary is written to support you in your Bible reading. It is designed to be read just once a week as you begin your Bible reading on Monday. Just as you may find help in appreciating a film, concert, or sporting event by reading program notes before the event, so you may find help in appreciating your Bible study for the week by reading the program notes offered in this book.

Comments are offered providing an overview of the readings in the Old Testament, epistle and gospel texts assigned for the week. These comments include some background on the theological and historical setting of the writings along with the rationale, where applicable, for reading the texts during the particular season. Comments are also offered when the text provides insight about the rites, hymns, customs of the church, or our calling to act for Christ in the world. This weekly guide differs from Forward Movement's *Forward Day by Day* series that often follows the daily lectionary. *Forward Day by Day* offers daily meditations on the readings while the weekly guide offers weekly overviews about the readings. Both resources are offered by Forward Movement to support you in your desire to understand and to be empowered by daily Bible reading.

A few notes for your consideration as you read this guide in the coming weeks:

• The Forward Movement *Daily Prayer and Bible Study with the Book of Common Prayer* will help you understand the context of the daily worship experience that goes with the Bible texts assigned in the lectionary.

• The daily lectionary readings are shown on pages 936-964 of the Episcopal *Book of Common Prayer*; on pages 452-475 of The Anglican Church of Canada, *The Book of Alternative Services,* and on pages 97-99 of the *Lutheran Book of Worship.*

• The daily lectionary follows a sequential pattern of reading scripture each day beginning Monday and running through

2

Saturday. With the exception of the Old Testament, the Sunday readings assigned in the daily lectionary usually have no connection whatsoever with the rest of the week. Therefore, only the readings appointed from the Old Testament for Sundays are considered.

• The psalms are read on a seven-week cycle. No attempt is made in this commentary to provide "program notes" on the psalms. The Oxford Annotated *Revised Standard Version* or *New English Bible* give excellent and brief explanations of the psalms. You may want to read the psalms from the annotated Bible rather than from your prayer book on occasion so that you can appreciate the finer points.

May scripture come alive for you as you become immersed in the world of the Bible with daily reading. May your life be empowered as you see more clearly the presence and power of God revealed through the pages of scripture. "For whatever was written in former days was written for our instruction, that by steadfastness and by the encouragement of the scriptures we might have hope." (Romans 15:4). We study the Bible not simply for an understanding of the past but for a clearer perception of how God is working in history and in creation today. This is what makes Bible study so exciting and so important for each Christian.

"Blessed Lord, who caused all holy Scriptures to be written for our learning: Grant us so to hear them, read, mark, learn and inwardly digest them, that we may embrace and ever hold fast the blessed hope of everlasting life, which you have given us in our Savior Jesus Christ; who lives and reigns with you and the Holy Spirit, one God for ever and ever." (BCP, p. 236) This collect was written by Thomas Cranmer for the first English prayer book, 1549. His deep concern was that the whole church become involved in Bible study. And so our quest continues this day following the well marked footprints of our ancestors in the faith. Enjoy!

Joseph P. Russell

Advent

Happy New Year! That is the appropriate greeting for Christians living within the liturgical church year, for this week we begin a new cycle of seasons, celebrations, festivals and selected lectionary readings. We turn from the last week of year 2 to begin reading with the first week of year 1.

Advent is a season that looks forward to the coming of Christ at the end of the age. At the same time we look forward, the season moves us back in our thinking to the time when our biblical ancestors were anticipating the coming of the new age of God to be ushered in by the Messiah. It is a season that blends a heavy emphasis of penance with anticipatory joy at the coming of the Lord. The joy, however, cannot be tasted without recognizing the bitterness of our sin. God will come to bring a new day, but God will also come to judge our present day. What have we done with the life the Lord has given us? This is the penitential question of Advent that we must consider before we move to greet the new day.

As we concluded our course of readings during the late weeks after Pentecost, we noted the increasingly "apocalyptic" nature of the selections. (See the comments in connection with the Book of Revelation, Proper 24.) Impending judgment and promise have been the themes expressed in our reading for several weeks. This increasingly apocalyptic message has also been a characteristic of the Sunday lectionary readings you've been hearing at the Eucharist. The church has been preparing us for the movement into Advent. The seasons of the liturgical church year follow the pattern set in the seasons of nature. We see signs of fall with the first turning of color, and then the fullness of fall arrives with colder winds that point, in turn, to winter. And so it is with our liturgical year. We see the colors of Advent forming with the late weeks after Pentecost that prepare us for the fullness of the Advent season that prepares us, in turn, for the wonder of Christmas.

The first week of Advent

The Old Testament readings:
Keep these remarks in mind as you begin your reading from the prophet, Isaiah, this week. Historically, we move in time to about 750 years before the time of Jesus. The once great kingdom of David had been split by a civil war in 938 B.C. resulting in two small, struggling nations, Israel in the north and Judah in the south. One enemy power after another threatened those two small nations, and they often struggled against each other in various alliances for power. As Isaiah wrote, the great nation of Assyria threatened Israel and Judah. Two characteristic responses shaped the people's thinking. On the one hand lay the desire to make foreign alliances to fight off the domination of the Assyrians. On the other lay the hope that God would at last protect his precious people because of his covenant made with them in the wilderness under Moses. The people looked forward to that intervention, that coming "day of the Lord."

Isaiah spoke out against both hopes. He spoke with painful words of judgment against a people he loved. The Lord looked for justice, but saw only oppression. The great day of the Lord that some look for will be a day of doom and judgment for the people, Isaiah warned. "Human pride will be humbled." (Isaiah 2:17)

Mixed with judgment are words of hope, a reminder that this is our Advent message, too. The Wednesday reading opens with a vision of the day when all nations will come to Jerusalem and God ". . .will wield authority over the nations." (Isaiah 2:4a) Saturday's reading includes a metaphor familiar to many of us. "That day, the branch of Yahweh shall be beauty and glory. . ." (Isaiah 4:2) God will renew his people. That is the promise of Isaiah. That, too, is the promise of Advent. The words of Isaiah that we read this Advent season lie at the heart of the Church's call to speak out in our day for social and economic justice. We, too, are warned, there can be no compromise with injustice.

5

The Epistle readings:

This week, we are exposed to the earliest writing of the New Testament with the reading of Paul's first letter to the Thessalonians. Acts 17 describes the context of Paul's brief visit in Thessalonika. Paul was on his second missionary journey. He and Silas had just been miraculously saved from imprisonment by an earthquake in Philippi. They then moved on to the city of Thessalonika where they again encountered difficulties with the Jewish authorities. After a short time, Paul was forced to leave the city and wend his way down to Athens and then on to Corinth. Though his visit at Thessalonika was short, Paul stayed long enough to establish a church firmly rooted in the Gospel he preached. While in Corinth (about 50 A.D.), he continued to think about his friends in Thessalonika. He sent Silas and Timothy back to Thessalonika to find out how the young church was doing. They returned to Paul in Corinth with good news—the Gospel had indeed taken root, but they also brought back a concern from the people about the "parousia" or return of Christ at the end of the age. "When is the end to come?", the people were asking, "and what happens to those among us who have already died? Will they be taken into the kingdom with Christ, or will they be left behind?" It is this concern for the end of the age that makes the letters to the Thessalonians appropriate for the Advent season.

Read the letter and feel both the hope and the pain that Paul must have felt.

The Gospel readings:

Our reading of the Gospel of Luke, begun in mid-September, continues into Advent. The chapter-by-chapter course readings become increasingly appropriate for the Advent season, for we hear the words of Jesus spoken after his entrance into Jerusalem. Facing his own suffering and death, he points ahead to the suffering, destruction and death that will come not only to his followers, but to all creation. The struggle is not the final word. The final word is the victory of Christ at the last day, in the resurrection of the dead and the transformation of all in the Lord.

Our week opens with increasing confrontation between Jesus and the Jewish authorities. It is this confrontation that leads to the cross, but Jesus faces both with grim determination. The parables he tells are parables of judgment against the nation. The Parable of the Wicked Husbandmen we read on Tuesday was "aimed at them," the scribes and chief priests realized. They are also "aimed at us," who are appointed in our time to care for the vineyard of the Lord.

Wednesday's reading is a familiar one. Jesus is asked about paying tribute to Caesar, with the hope of trapping him. "Render to Caesar" is not a license for civil government to have unlimited authority in this world. So long as civil authorities do not act against God's will, then we may act in obedience to them, but God always remains our ultimate authority, demanding an obedience that transcends state, society and even family prerogative.

Friday's reading about Christ being the son of David is confusing without a knowledge of the context of the psalm and sonship of King David. The point of the reading is that Jesus' role in history and eternity cannot be pinned down merely to being a son of King David. He is the expected Messiah, but a Messiah far greater than Israel's greatest king.

Saturday's reading will remind you of our time spent in the Book of Revelation. The poetry of apocalyptic permeates Jesus' words here as we read of great earthquakes and mysterious signs of the final times. Persecution and trial are the roads to salvation, Jesus warns, but through it all, Christians will know in every age that the Lord walks with them.

The second week of Advent

The Old Testament readings:

The feeling of judgment that is such a part of the Advent message is inherent in the Isaiah passages for this week.

We begin on Sunday with the Song of the Vineyard. Isaiah probably took a familiar ballad sung in the vineyards of Judah at harvest time, but he added a surprise ending, meant to shock the listener into realizing the decadence that Judah had fallen into. The Lord had planted Israel and had expected a great harvest of justice and shalom. Instead, all he got were the "sour grapes" of oppression and injustice. Jesus may well have had this poem in mind as he told the Parable of the Wicked Husbandmen.

The Song of the Vineyard sets the mood for the rest of the week. On Monday and Tuesday, we read why Isaiah felt that Judah was yielding only "wild grapes." "Woe to those who add house to house" is the first of six woes of wrong doing. See how the theme of social justice heads the list of national sins. Some got richer at the expense of others. The covenant made with Israel in the wilderness assumed equal holdings of land. Verses 26-30 of chapter 5 are not assigned for our reading, but they describe, in frightening clarity, the punishment that would come for Judah's unfaithfulness.

On Wednesday we'll read familiar words. The sanctus from the Holy Eucharist, "Holy, holy, holy Lord, God of power and might, heaven and earth are full of your glory," comes from this vision of Isaiah. At the Holy Eucharist, each of us is given a vision of God's kingdom for, as we come to the Lord's table, it is like stepping momentarily into the kingdom of heaven where we join in the eternal chorus of praise with "Angels and archangels and with the company of heaven..."

Isaiah's vision gave him a sense of calling. He was to go and speak to the people in the Lord's name, but he must have realized at that moment of being consecrated and set apart for God's work, that his mission would not be successful.

We see deafness to God's word happening at the highest levels of Judean life. Some five years after Isaiah's vision, he tried to embolden King Uzziah's grandson, Ahaz. "Don't worry about the threatened invasion of Aram and Israel (also referred to in these passages as Ephraim). Before they can invade, they will be laid waste. Trust me. "Ask me for a sign to guarantee my word that Aram and Israel will not touch you," was the message of God spoken through Isaiah. But Ahaz refused to ask for a sign, proving to Isaiah that he lacked faith in God. Worse yet, Ahaz appealed to Assyria for help against his enemies Aram and Israel. Rather than rely on the Lord, he tried to rely on the very nation that would destroy him. Because Ahaz refused a sign of hope, he'd receive a sign of doom, Isaiah warned. Even now, a young woman was pregnant. Before the child was old enough to know the difference between good and evil, Assyria would sweep through Judah and destroy the once proud land. Curds and honey were the food of nomadic tribes and not the food of a settled people. Poverty and suffering were imminent.

The words about the young maiden are familiar to us. Matthew quoted from this passage in pointing to the significance of Mary's pregnancy. Here the pregnancy and birth of a child to a young maiden are a sign of imminent destruction, but Matthew saw Mary's pregnancy as a sign of eternal hope for all people.

Another birth is announced in Saturday's reading. This time it is a child born to a prophetess who conceived and gave birth to a son who was then given a symbolic name. Again, the threat leveled against Israel for unfaithfulness was an invasion by Assyria. "The wealth of Damascus and the booty of Samaria will be carried off by the King of Assyria." (Isaiah 8:4)

The Epistle readings:
We conclude the reading of Paul's first letter to the Thessalonians on Tuesday. Read carefully the description of the day of the Lord. It will come quietly "like a thief in the night" with no signs or warning.

9

On Wednesday we begin the reading of the second letter to the Thessalonians. Many scholars question whether this is a genuine letter of Paul. In biblical times, it was customary for a disciple of a great teacher to write under his master's name. The language and the imagery of the second letter are certainly different. The Book of Revelation that we read a couple of weeks ago may come to mind. Notice the strong words of revenge. Those persecuting the church will pay the price in the end. The message about the coming of Christ seems to be a direct contradiction to the first letter. The day won't come as a thief in the night. Rather, the day will be introduced by many dramatic signs.

The Gospel readings:

The weeks we spent in the Book of Revelation have prepared us for our apocalyptic Advent readings. The message of apocalyptic writing is that the people of God will inevitably suffer for witnessing to God's action in the world. The terrible suffering, however, will end in victory for the faithful. The suffering is the trial that leads to fullness in the kingdom of God.

The application for us is that we must be alert and ready for the Lord's return. There is meaning to our life's struggles. We dare not compromise the call for justice and transformation demanded by the Gospel. To do so is to surrender to the principalities and powers of the present age.

Advent is far more than a preparation for Christmas and the celebration of the birth of Jesus in a manger. Advent is a time when the church is called to point to a life and ethic that transcends the demands of the present age. We live in the world, as Jesus said, but we are not of this world. Our ethical standards for the individual and society must be higher than the ethical demands of the world at large, because our lives are meant to point to the coming of God's kingdom. No wonder Jesus warned of trial and controversy in this life.

On Wednesday we seem to be stepping for a moment into the Gospel of John. However, some ancient manuscripts place

John 7:53-8:11 right after Luke 21:38, leading many biblical scholars to feel that the passage belongs with Luke rather than John. Your Bible may not include this passage at all, because of the confusion surrounding it.

We move into more familiar territory, beginning on Thursday, as we start the reading of the passion narrative. The passion was Jesus' trial that led to his glorification. We associate the narrative with Holy Week, but if we are to appreciate the fullness of the Advent season, we need to move with Jesus into an awareness of what his coming into our lives may mean ultimately for us as Christians.

The third week of Advent

The Old Testament readings:

Our week opens with a striking reference to the day of the Lord. This was a term used by Isaiah to describe a time when the Lord would intervene in history to destroy Judah's enemies and bring victory for the kingdom of God. The enemies to be destroyed in this case were Babylonia, Assyria, and Philistia. Those nations would be terrified at the Lord's coming.

On Monday we return to our chapter-by-chapter course reading of Isaiah, picking up where we left off on Saturday. Isaiah will "bind up this testimony" and leave it for his disciples to open his words for the generations to come. The testimony he is binding up are portions of the Book of Isaiah, chapters 1 through 39. Isaiah and his disciples were to be signs of God's activity among the people. His words are very similar to Jesus' words, expressed in John 13:33, 35. This passage and the passage from John, make a good purpose statement for the church of Christ.

Your feelings of Christmas may be touched on Tuesday morning, as you read the familiar words of Isaiah 9. "The people that walked in darkness have seen a great light." We may be reading a fragment of a royal inaugural liturgy used as the kings of Judah took the throne. The liturgical poem gives hope for the king who takes the throne, but in more idealistic terms it describes a perfect king who will come in David's lineage. This king will bring in a reign of perfect freedom from want, from oppression and from war. As Christians looked back at this poem, they realized the hope was met in Jesus.

On Wednesday and Thursday we turn from the great words that speak of the light of hope back to grim words describing imminent darkness. God's anger at the present situation is again expressed by Isaiah. Legislators enact oppressive laws. They refuse justice and cheat the poor.

Assyria receives God's wrath in Friday's reading. The king of Assyria would get his retribution, Isaiah warned, because

12

he boasted in his own strength, not realizing that the Lord was giving him his power in order to punish Israel and Judah. Because Assyria strutted with pride, the Lord would bring it down to the dust in humility.

We end the week on a hopeful note. A remnant of Judah will return to a devastated land and the mighty God will protect them.

The Epistle readings:
During the first half of Advent, we have been reading the earliest of the epistles in the New Testament. This week we move to the last epistles to be included in the collection. Second Peter could have been written as late as 140 A.D. Someone who was influenced by the followers of the apostle Peter, rather than the apostle himself, was probably the author.

The message of the writer is crucial. Christ has not returned. False teachers have come into the Christian communities with doctrines and interpretations of Christian writings that are leading people astray. Remember the promise of Christ, the writer urges. Don't lose hope in the Lord's return. You have a special calling as God's servant.

At the conclusion of Tuesday's reading, notice the warning about interpreting scripture. The individual cannot be trusted to understand scripture alone. This passage is one of the justifications the church used for many generations in attempting to control the reading and interpretation of scripture.

On Friday we leave 2 Peter and pick up a few verses of the Epistle of Jude. This is appropriate since the two epistles were written at about the same time and deal with the same problems that had arisen in the second century church. "Stay with your teaching and faith as the solid foundation of your life," is the message of Jude.

We, too, grow tired, disillusioned, and are led astray into false teachings. Advent calls us back to the path and to the vision.

The Gospel readings:

Our reading of the passion narrative continues on Monday and Tuesday, but the reading concludes with the words of Jesus spoken before the Sanhedrin that he will be ". . . seated at the right hand of the power of God." (Luke 22:69) The suffering of Jesus leads to his triumph, a model for the whole church to follow and an understanding of Christian life that is emphasized in the Advent readings.

The daily readings from Wednesday through Saturday will add dimension to the Sunday celebration of word and sacrament, since John the Baptist is the focus of the Sunday gospel for the second and third Sundays of Advent. John came to prepare the way for Christ. The role of the church is to prepare the way for Christ to come again. As John pointed beyond himself to one whose sandals he was not fit ". . . to kneel down and undo. . .", so we must point beyond ourselves to the Christ.

Friday's reading provides us with an evaluation of our life as the church of Christ. John's disciples ask Jesus if he is in fact the one who is expected. Jesus' reply does not talk about how many disciples he has or how eloquently he has been preaching God's word. Jesus' reply focuses on acts of healing and transformation, powerful signs of God's reign pointed out by Isaiah. (Isaiah 35:5-6) We who are the church are called out by Christ to continue the birth process that he began.

The fourth week of Advent

Note: The length of this liturgical week will vary according to the day on which Christmas falls. Use the readings for December 24 on the day before Christmas regardless of what day of the week it is.

The Old Testament readings:

Our week begins with great words of vision and hope. On Sunday we move into the writings of Deutero-Isaiah, a second major prophet who lived during the Babylonian exile, around the years 586 through 538 B.C. His writings were included on the same scroll as the prophet Isaiah, who wrote in the eighth century before Christ. Sunday's reading is the first of four Songs of the Servant of God, found in the writings of Deutero-Isaiah. All four poems describe the perfect ruler of Israel, whose suffering will redeem all the peoples of the world. In Isaiah 42:7 we read he is appointed ". . .to open the eyes that are blind, to bring captives out of prison. . ." This servant ". . .will never waver, nor be crushed until true justice is established on earth. . ." (Isaiah 42:4) These words are applied by the early church to Jesus, and they describe the role the church must take in every generation.

The visionary words of hope continue into Monday's reading with a selection which may also be familiar, for it has long been associated with the readings heard in early Advent. A new king is coming who is from the "stock of Jesse," (The family of Jesse) the father of King David. This king will have God's spirit resting upon him, and he will bring great gifts of the Spirit to the people. Seven gifts are named in Isaiah 11:2, the same gifts that are enumerated in the prayer offered at the time of baptism. (See BCP, p. 308.) This king will usher in the perfect reign of God, a time when paradise shall be restored. Poetic imagery describes the kingdom: "The wolf will lie down with the lamb" and all creation shall be at peace. Christmas card imagery comes to mind, for we associate this section with the birth of Jesus.

Hopeful words continue with Tuesday's vision of a second exodus. Just as the Lord led the Israelites out of Egyptian slavery under the guidance of Moses, so God's people will be led "dry-shod" back to restoration from captivity. Their days of punishment over, the people will be brought home in peace.

The parallel themes of Advent continue in our reading this final week. On the one hand, visions of hope and power are offered, but on the other hand, we are reminded over and over that God's coming means earth-shaking judgment. The readings for Wednesday, Thursday and Friday return us to the judgment theme. Wednesday's reading is taken from the midst of Isaiah's bitter words spoken against those who have taunted him for his doomsday preaching. His taunters, Isaiah claims, ridicule him by mimicking words that are meaningless to them, "Blah, blah, blah" or "sav lason, sav lason." (Isaiah 28:10) Isaiah's bitter adversaries may have actually used such taunts against him as he attempted to preach the words he felt called to say. They will hear those same taunting words again, Isaiah warned. But this time the words will come from the Assyrians as they are led away as captives, and the people still won't understand!

Thursday's reading continues the condemnation of false alliances and includes a denunciation of empty "memorized" worship. Such formalized worship is no substitute for the following of God's law of justice and integrity.

On Friday and Saturday, our hopeful theme returns. We hear again of the blind seeing and the "ears of the deaf unsealed." God's peace is coming and so is the great festival of peace that is Christmas.

The Epistle readings:

The Book of Revelation appropriately becomes our focal point these final days before Christmas. "Christ has died. Christ is risen. Christ will come again" is the proclamation we make at the Eucharist. Advent prepares us for the "Christ will come again" part of that proclamation by first looking back at the expectations our biblical ancestors of Old Testament times had about the coming Messiah. It then looks ahead to the expectations the church has always held for the return of Christ to usher in the kingdom or reign of God.

In the Book of Revelation we read vivid poetic imagery this week that is not to be literalized. The major purpose of this book was to give hope to those who faced persecution and who mourned the deaths of the martyrs. Such people, we read on Monday, are to be the first who are rewarded. Christ will come and reign for 1,000 years, and the martyrs will be a part of his victorious reign. Then Christ will emerge victorious from the last battle against Satan, and a new heaven and a new earth and a new Jerusalem will descend to earth. The sea, which represented evil and fear to the ancients, will be dried up and all suffering will end. Now the rest of those who have remained faithful to Christ will join the martyrs in one eternal, glorious song of praise to God.

The Gospel readings:

Our Gospel readings move us right into the celebration of Christmas. We begin on Monday with a selection from the Gospel of John. The context is Jesus' discourse with the Jews who rejected his sign of power when he cured the sick man at the pool of Bethesda. Instead of seeing in the healing a sign of God's presence among them, they were upset because the healing happened on the Sabbath!

The rest of this week of Advent we read Luke's account of the events leading up to Jesus' birth. Mary's song, the Magnificat, read Thursday, speaks about the radical nature of God's transforming action in history that is made known to Jesus. "He has pulled down princes from their thrones and exalted the lowly. The hungry he has filled with good things, the rich sent empty away." (Luke 1:52-53) God's Kingdom means a reversal and a transformation of the present order, and the church is to participate in that transformation.

Christmas Day and the following week

The day of the week that Christmas falls on determines the readings you use in this season. Christmas Day has an appointed set of readings, page 940, Book of Common Prayer. The three days following Christmas Day are the feast day of St. Stephen on December 26, the feast day of St. John on December 27 and the feast day of the Holy Innocents on December 28. You will find readings appointed for those special days on page 996. Then, on December 29, return to the daily lectionary for the week following Christmas Day, on page 940. Follow the week's readings to December 31, which is also the Eve of the Feast of the Holy Name.

The Old Testament readings:
All of our readings this week are appropriately great hymns of praise and thanksgiving to God for his mighty acts. Tuesday's reading, the first five verses of Isaiah 25, area victory hymn sung at the fall of an enemy city. The second half of the reading is a joyful hymn that looks forward to the great "messianic banquet," a metaphor of perfect happiness with God when the kingdom is finally proclaimed. All peoples will gather with the Lord at his banquet table, rejoicing in their salvation. Tears will be wiped away forever. This poetic image of the fulfillment of God's kingdom played an important role in Jesus' mind as he celebrated the Last Supper with his disciples. "I tell you, I shall not drink wine until the day I drink the new wine with you in the kingdom of my Father," Jesus said as he took the cup. (Mt. 26:29) This is a clear reference to the messianic banquet. Each time we participate in the Holy Eucharist, we have a foretaste of that great banquet. We step into the kingdom for a moment and experience the presence of God together. The unseen guests at the table are those who have gone before us and who already enjoy the fullness of the banquet. When we sing or say the Sanctus at the Holy Eucharist, we preface the hymn with these words: "Therefore

we praise you, joining our voices with Angels and Archangels and with all the company of heaven, who forever sing this hymn to proclaim the glory of your Name." Our voices join in one great eternal chorus, a rehearsal for the chorus of the kingdom fulfilled.

The Epistle readings:

The epistle readings appointed for December 29, 30 and 31, point out the full meaning of the Feast of the Nativity of Our Lord or Christmas Day. The readings move our concentration on the infant Jesus in a manger to the meaning of his birth and life among us. Jesus the Christ came to reveal the mysteries of God's saving action in creation. He came to reconcile the whole world to God and to begin a new creation in every person who enters into Christ's life. This Jesus, whose birth we celebrate, is the "alpha and the omega," the first and the last, and this Jesus will return at the end of the age as the triumphant Christ.

The Gospel readings:

To accept Jesus as the Savior is to know Jesus as the living water and as the light of the world. These metaphors touch the reality of our life in Christ. Jesus is the true water that will lead to life. Those who thirst for life and seek the light of the knowledge of God, can turn to the Christ whose birth is celebrated in this season. These readings also point ahead to the rejection that came so soon in Jesus' life, a rejection that points ahead to the Holy Week and Good Friday. Christmas must always be celebrated within the shadow of the cross.

The first week in January

This first week in January we follow the numbered days of the month, rather than the days of the week. Though we call the Sundays between Christmas and Epiphany the first and second Sundays after Christmas, traditionally the whole 12 days between Christmas and the Feast of the Epiphany (January 6) are considered the season of Christmas. The familiar Christmas carol, "The Twelve Days of Christmas," reflects this ancient liturgical practice.

Christmas is far more than the celebration of the birth of Jesus in Bethlehem. With the birth of Jesus, we recognize that God came to dwell with us in the flesh of a human being. People truly saw God in the man, Jesus.

Where is God?

God is right here, in this person.

How do we know?

Because, when we are in the presence of this man, we feel as if we are in the presence of God. His actions with us and for us restore, liberate, and transform us and call us into being as new creatures. We can feel that happening to us. We can see it happening among us. With Jesus, God became incarnate; this is God become flesh. That's what the word incarnate means.

But more than that. Jesus promised that when he died he would still be with us in the flesh of our human existence. Now God would dwell within us through the power of the Holy Spirit so that we would continue to meet God in the flesh and blood encounters of life.

The Old Testament readings:

We get four distinct scenes depicting times when God revealed himself to our biblical ancestors. In Matthew 1:23 we are reminded of the words of the prophet in Isaiah 7:14: "The virgin (or young maiden) will conceive and give birth to a son, and they will call him Immanuel." The name Immanuel is one of the names we give to Jesus. It means "God with us." That is the theme of these four pictures of God's revelation of himself to our biblical ancestors in Old Testament times. The message in each of the scenes is the same: "God is with you." Notice, especially in Genesis 28, the promises God gave to our forefather, Jacob. God will be with Jacob, God will keep him safe and God will bring him home. Those promises are the same as those made to us through Jesus the Christ.

The Epistle readings:

The epistle readings this week are all taken from Hebrews 11. This is one long beautiful reminder that the great men and women of the Old Testament lived in faith for a promise that they never saw fulfilled. (Incidentally, verses 8-16 are assigned for reading on Independence Day. Notice how appropriate this whole section is to our nation's history.) The promise that our Old Testament ancestors did not live to see is Jesus Christ. The readings for the week end with a reminder that we must not "...lose sight of Jesus." And yet we must live in faith, too, for the final kingdom that Christ ushered in still remains to be completed. We live in faith that Jesus "...has taken his place at the right of God's throne." (Hebrews 12:2)

The Gospel readings:

What does Jesus' birth mean to us who enter into covenant with God through him? The Gospel readings give us metaphors that provide us with parameters of faith:

January 2—Jesus is the bread of life. "He who comes to me will never be hungry." (John 6:35) Whoever sees Jesus and believes in him has eternal life, and a faith response is called for. We must not pack Jesus away with our Christmas ornaments until next year. We must see and respond in order to inherit the promise.

January 3—Jesus has come so that we may have life.

January 4—Jesus is the "Way, the Truth, and the Life." To have seen Jesus is to have seen God.

January 5—Jesus is the true vine, and we are the branches. Our life comes out of that vine.

The great Feast of the Epiphany is our next marker along the way that is the liturgical year. Old Testament, psalm, and epistle selections are offered for the evening before the feast day.

The Epiphany and following

The numbered days we will use in the week set forth on the top of page 942 of the Book of Common Prayer will vary according to when the Saturday evening following the feast of the Epiphany falls.

The word, "Epiphany," comes from the Greek word meaning "to show forth" or "to reveal." The word was used in Jesus' time to describe the appearance of a monarch before the people: "The king made his epiphany last week and talked about his foreign policies to the assembled people." In an epiphany, the ruler would reveal himself and his ideas and expectations to the people. We say that Jesus was an epiphany of God in much the same sense. God in Jesus revealed his nature, his love and his new covenant to the people. Moreover, the church is called to make the same kind of epiphany to the world.

The Epiphany season is a time of looking back in order to recognize how God is working in the present moment.

Because the date of Easter varies, the Epiphany season can be as long as eight weeks or as short as four weeks.

The Old Testament readings:

Our Old Testmanet readings this week are from the second part of the book of the prophet Isaiah. The first part of the book was written by Isaiah before the Babylonian exile. Beginning with chapter 40, we are introduced to the second and perhaps a third prophet who wrote during the exile and after the return to the homeland. Scholars often refer to "Trito" or "third" Isaiah as an author of the final chapters of this great book. All of these writings were placed on the same scroll, and thus are found in the same book.

The theme that we read this week is the theme of how God was revealed to Israel, and to us, in the history of our people. God came to an oppressed and exiled people and led them to freedom. God will come at a final day of the Lord to reveal his name to all peoples and bring some to judgment and others to a realization of God's eternal promise. God comes in every age to bring judgment to the oppressors and liberation to the oppressed. God redeems or restores those suffering at the hand of an enemy.

Here is the way the theme unfolds during the week:

Feast of The Epiphany—God is revealed as peace, happiness and salvation by a messenger proclaiming the victory of God to the people. Picture the scene that this poem presents. A runner comes to proclaim the Good News. The watchmen on the city gates repeat it to the people. All the world will see the victory of God.

January 7—God is revealed in the redemption or restoration of the people. The exiles at last shall know the Lord's name and shall realize that the Lord is indeed with them. (A thought that picks up the theme from Christmas, "Emmanuel—God with us.")

January 8—God comes armed with integrity, salvation and vengeance, as a redeemer of his people. The "armor of God" metaphor is reflected beautifully in Paul's writings. (See Ephesians 6:14-17 and 1 Thessalonians 5:8)

January 9—Keep the well known words of "Battle Hymn of the Republic" in mind as you read from Isaiah 63. God returns from battle victorious with the blood of those who oppressed his people—splattered on him. God has punished Edom, symbolic of all nations and people who oppose the Lord.

January 10—God will be revealed through the act of saving a small remnant of people in time of destructive upheaval.

January 11—This remnant, saved from destruction by God, will shame those who refused to keep covenant with the Lord. The remnant will be given a new name and will receive their blessing from God. As the early church, including St. Paul, thought about passages such as this, they began to identify with the faithful remnant.

January 12—Our series of epiphany poems ends with a tremendous poem that describes a day when there will be a new heaven and a new earth created by God.

The Epistle readings:

The church is called to be a part of God's epiphany to the world. The test of how faithful we are in our covenant with Christ is scored by how we have revealed the Lord's mercy, forgiveness, compassion and healing to the world. The letters of the seven churches of Asia, from the Book of Revelation, makes a good epiphany score card for us today. The writer of Revelation speaks of lukewarmness, a loss of love for the Lord, and other accusations as he reflects on the witness of the churches. These letters serve as a prologue for the rest of the book. Our faithfulness to the covenant will indeed be judged, warns the writer of Revelation.

The Gospel readings:

In the readings assigned for the week following the feast of the Epiphany, six of the seven great signs of Christ's revelation are presented in the Gospel of John. The last of the signs, assigned for January 12, sums up the Epiphany season for us. Having seen the mighty works of God revealed in Christ (in this case, bringing sight to a man born blind), what are we to do about it?

The selections assigned on the top half of page 942 of the Book of Common Prayer are followed until the evening before the first Sunday after the Epiphany. After the first Sunday, move down to the bottom half of the page for the week following.

The week of 1 Epiphany

The Old Testament readings:

We've been reading from Isaiah since the beginning of Advent, but this week we move into the writings of Deutero, or Second Isaiah, who wrote almost 200 years later, during the Babylonian exile.

During the seasons of Advent and Christmas we read from First Isaiah the threats of coming doom and God's call for repentance to a recalcitrant people. Second Isaiah's concern was to speak to a people suffering under the punishment of exile. He wanted to give them courage and a sense of hope that God would act soon. "Comfort, comfort my people says your God." Those opening words of Second Isaiah set the theme for the whole work of the prophet. Judah is now to be comforted after her punishment of exile. The prophet takes us into the courtroom of God where future plans are announced to the heavenly beings. A wilderness highway is to be prepared for the people so that they can return home. Though everything else may fall and die, God's word is eternal.

The majesty and creative power of God is compared with the utter impotence of the gods of the other nations that are fashioned by craftsmen. The words we read on Monday are biting words of cynicism aimed at the gods that so many Jews were tempted to worship in the strange land of Babylonia.

On Wednesday we are called with the nations of the world into the courtroom where God is the judge. "Listen to me in silence, O coastlands...let them approach, then let them speak; let us together draw near for judgment" are the words that Second Isaiah gives God to speak as bailiff and judge of the heavenly court. What other god could raise a victorious king "from the east" who would soon defeat the Babylonians and restore the Jews to their homeland? That is the question for the court to decide. The king referred to is Cyrus of Persia who was indeed moving victoriously across the ancient world. Unlike most of the rulers of this day, Cyrus was a generous victor.

He allowed captive people to return to their homeland. Second Isaiah could see the day when Babylonia would fall to Cyrus who would then open the way for the return of the people. In the midst of Wednesday's reading we see Israel referred to as God's servant. Keep that phrase in mind for we will see it again in the coming days.

In Thursday's reading we hear of a new creation that is coming. The desert will bloom. Water shall flow into pools of the wilderness. A whole new created order is happening that rivals the first creation described in Genesis. Second Isaiah returns to the ridicule of the worthless gods of the other nations that are nothing more than images made by people.

The servant theme returns again in Friday's reading. Verses 1-9 of chapter 42 are optional, but I would suggest you read them. "Behold my servant, whom I uphold..." Though Christians have traditionally identified these words as applying to Jesus, the context of all the servant psalms taken together would suggest that Second Isaiah had in mind the Jewish people, the nation that God had called out of Egypt. Though Cyrus would win victory through sword and battle, Judah will bring justice quietly not even bruising the reeds as she moves across the land. The role of this servant is spelled out in verses 5 through 9.

Midway through Friday's reading, the imagery shifts from the servant nation to warrior God. God who has called forth Israel to act in history now acts himself. His patience has run out. A new day of victory for God's justice is about to dawn. Second Isaiah next presents God as a woman in labor about to give birth to the new creation. Notice the female as well as male imagery.

In the 33rd chapter of Exodus there is a beautiful passage in which Moses begs God to send someone with him to lead the people through the wilderness. The response that Moses receives from God is significant. "My presence will go with you, and I will give you rest...you have found favor in my sight and I know you by name." (Exodus 33:14, 17). In Saturday's reading this promise is repeated. God knows Isreal by name and God will never abandon the people.

The Epistle readings:

We begin the sequential reading of Ephesians on Monday. Christ came "to unite all things to him, things in heaven and things on earth." That is the hidden mystery revealed to the Christians. The letter of Paul to the Ephesians appears to have been written by a disciple of Paul rather than by the apostle Paul himself. It may have been written as an introductory statement to the whole body of Paul's letters as they circulated among the various congregations he had established. Compare Ephesians to Corinthians to see the contrast with a letter known to be written by Paul. One of the reasons Paul's authorship is doubted is that though the apostle spent considerable time in the city, this epistle lacks any real sense of familiarity between the writer and the recipients.

The power of God's free grace revealed in Christ is the theme of Wednesday's text. We have been created through our baptism to carry out the work God has called us to do. Thus, we do not act in order to earn our righteousness before God. Rather our righteous actions for Christ come as a result of the free grace bestowed upon us as disciples.

The generations of enmity and separation between Jew and gentile are ended in Christ. Jew and gentile are now one.

Great words of peace are expressed in Thursday's reading. The follower of Christ becomes a part of the living temple of God.

Saturday's reading ends with one of the concluding doxologies used in Morning and Evening Prayer: "Glory to God whose power, working in us, can do infinitely more than we can ask or imagine; Glory to him from generation to generation in the church, and in Christ Jesus for ever and ever." (Ephesians 3:20-21, BCP pp. 102 and 126).

The Gospel readings:

We begin our reading of the Gospel of Mark on Monday. This gospel may have been written for the church in Rome, but that remains conjecture. The Temple in Jerusalem had been leveled by Roman armies as they crushed the last attempts of Jewish

Zealots to overthrow foreign rule. Moreover, the church was undergoing persecution. Christians were scattering as conditions in Jerusalem grew worse.

In this painful historic situation, the writer of the Gospel of Mark collected the stories of Jesus that he knew and wove them into a proclamation of Good News. The basic message: have hope, for the agony of the present time is the dawning of the age of fulfillment that is coming soon. The core of Mark's Gospel is that those who keep faith in this Good News will share both in the suffering and in the glory of the risen Christ.

Mark loses no time getting into the message of the gospel. No birth story precedes the ministry of Jesus. John appears in the wilderness as a rustic Elijah figure to announce the new age. Jesus comes up out of the waters of his baptism to be led into the wilderness where he, unlike his ancestors in the Sinai wilderness, overcomes the temptations of evil.

The authority of Jesus to drive out evil, to teach, and to call disciples, is expressed with power in our reading for Tuesday.

The Jewish people at the time of Jesus, yearned for the ushering in of the messianic age. Evil would be defeated and God's kingdom would triumph. This expectation of the triumphant ending of the present age of darkness, with the coming of God's kingdom, framed the hopes and expectations of the Jewish people. They dreamed of a new David and a new kingdom. In the prophetic poetry found in the Book of Daniel, a figure is introduced in Daniel 7:13 who comes to usher in God's new age: "I saw in the night visions, and behold, with the clouds of heaven there came one like a son of man, and he came to the Ancient of Days and was presented to him..." One of Mark's purposes in writing his Gospel was to point out over and over again, that this triumphant Son of Man, who was expected at the coming of the new age was, in fact, Jesus.

Evil, sickness and death were all the dominion of the kingdom of Satan. Jesus' healings and exorcisms were signs that the victory of the kingdom of light over the kingdom of darkness had begun.

Only God could forgive sins. Temple priests could accept offerings for the forgiveness of sins, but even they could not pronounce the restoration. Jesus spoke as God when he stated forgiveness and healing to a paralytic lowered to him through the roof of a home. Such a statement would be blasphemy to a Jew. We cannot blame the scribes and Pharisees for their shocked response. Jesus spoke words reserved for God.

Because Jesus acted with the authority of Messiah, he could change the laws of Torah (the first five books of Hebrew Scripture). This is a new age that cannot be contained within the old, he pronounced. "No one sews a piece of unshrunk cloth on an old garment...no one puts new wine into old wineskins..." (Mark 2:21-22).

The week of 2 Epiphany

The Old Testament readings:
The people of Judah need dwell no more on memories, we read as our week in Second Isaiah begins on Sunday. God is bringing about a new Exodus even more magnificent than the Exodus that liberated Israel from the Egyptians. Cyrus of Persia will be the liberator this time as he moves against the Babylonians and defeats them. The covenant people do not deserve the Exodus, for they were not faithful to God, and yet God will restore them nevertheless. The writer moves between offering promises of the coming great day and denouncing the worthless gods of the surrounding nations.

Life in Babylonian exile was not necessarily hard for the people of Judah, and many of them were awed by the magnificence of Babylonian culture as they compared it with their own. Tuesday's reading is a parody in which Second Isaiah ridicules the idol worship of the Babylonians.

In sharp contrast to the description of the worthless idols of Babylon, Wednesday's lection describes the mighty acts of God in creation and in history. Cyrus of Persia is to be God's "shepherd" who will lead Israel back home. We are accustomed to thinking of Israel's kings as being the anointed ones and the shepherds of Israel. Now we discover that this foreign ruler who does not even know the God of Israel is to be the anointed shepherd of God's people. Here we see another major movement in Israel's understanding of God's power. Second Isaiah lifts Israel's understanding of God beyond the boundaries of nation and ancestry. With words of poetry, the prophet paints a new and broader universe so that the people can see the magnificence of a wider creation than they had ever imagined.

Israel may want to question the historic purposes of God, but can the clay question the potter? Thursday's text sounds like the words of God spoken to Job who had railed against the injustice of a righteous man suffering from disease and disgrace. "Were you there when I created the heavens and the earth," God asks Job at the conclusion of the Book of Job? And so Israel must bow to the wisdom of God.

Just as he raised the people's vision of how God acted in creation and in history, so Second Isaiah in Thursday's reading raises their vision of God's role in bringing salvation. It is not just to Israel that God comes as savior, but to all the nations of the world: "Turn to me and be saved, all the ends of the earth! For I am God, and there is no other. By myself I have sworn, from my mouth has gone forth in righteousness, a word that shall not return: 'To me every knee shall bow, every tongue shall swear,'" (Isaiah 45:22-23).

In exile, Israel can see a wider world and gain a wider understanding of the majesty and power of the God who called them into covenant so many years ago. Second Isaiah helps them to see the universal role of God and to see their own role as servants of God. They are to be a "light to the nations" in pointing the way of God to all peoples.

Our week in Second Isaiah ends with further words of utter disdain and ridicule for the gods in Babylon, Bel and Nebo. Babylon's gods must be carried in procession by the people, but Israel's God carries the people to safety.

The Epistle readings:

The opening versicles for Holy Baptism (BCP, p. 299) are taken directly from Ephesians 4, read on Monday: "There is one body and one spirit. . ." This statement echoes the creedal statement of the Jews as they recite the Shema from the Book of Deuteronomy: "Hear, O Israel: The Lord our God is one Lord; and you shall love the Lord your God with all your heart, and with all your soul, and with all your might." (Deut. 6:4). The writer of Ephesians proclaims the oneness that the Christian can know through Christ. There is a complete unity in God who is the source of everything.

Monday's text includes a quotation from Psalm 68 which the author uses to express the full ministry of Christ: "When he ascended on high he led a host of captives, and he gave gifts to men." (Ephesians 4:8, paraphrase of Psalm 68:18). Though the psalm spoke of Moses ascending the mountain of Sinai to bring down the gifts of the covenant, the author of Ephesians sees the text as referring to Christ who ascended to the heavens and brought the gifts of the Spirit to the Christians.

In the fifth chapter of Ephesians the writer outlines norms for Christian behavior in the home and in the world. If Christians are to witness to Christ's love in the world, then their lives must reflect that love in everything they say and do and in everything they refrain from doing.

Thursday's reading includes the oft quoted words about wives being obedient to their husbands and husbands honoring their wives. The point of the passage is to remind the church that they are to live subject to Christ. They live no longer for themselves, but for Christ. Moreover, the marriage of man and woman to each other expresses the close bond between Christ and the church. Marriage becomes metaphor expressing our relationship with God. As the preface to the marriage rite in the Book of Common Prayer says: "The bond and covenant of marriage was established by God in creation...It signifies to us the mystery of the union between Christ and his Church, and Holy Scripture commends it to be honored among all people." (BCP, 423). This is the point of Ephesians 5. We lose the point if we see the chapter as divine law establishing a hierarchical relationship in which the husband is always the head of the family and the woman is always second to the man.

The gifts of the Holy Spirit enable us to put off the old nature and put on the new. This results in a reorientation of our actions that are now turned toward Christ. Christians must continue to put on the "complete armor" of the risen Christ if we are to avoid the temptations, the struggles and the entrapments of the present age. The priest's putting on vestments for the liturgy symbolizes the putting on of the armor of God on behalf of the whole people of God.

The Gospel readings:

A surprising statement is read on Tuesday: ". . . but whoever blasphemes against the Holy Spirit never has forgiveness, but is guilty of eternal sin." (Mark 3:29). Though we cannot know exactly what Jesus had in mind when he made this statement, it is evident that one cannot be healed and forgiven by the Spirit if one denies the power of the Spirit.

In the middle of the week, Jesus is teaching a crowd of people by the lake side. He must step into a boat in order to move far enough out from the people to be seen and heard by them. Jesus proceeds to tell three parables, all with a similar point: the parable of the sower, the parable of the seed growing by itself, and the parable of the mustard seed. God is bringing in the kingdom. (The presence and power of Jesus is proof enough of that.) Though we may now barely discern the kingdom, it will come in its own good time, and its fulfillment will be beyond our wildest expectations.

Part of Mark's concern in writing this Gospel was to deal with the question that bothered the church of his time: "Why were not more people convinced that Jesus was the Messiah when his miracles and powerful acts of new life should have been so obvious to everyone?" Part of the explanation, Mark believed, lay in the hidden nature of Jesus' words and acts. (Read Mark 4:9-12.) It was God's will that the word would remain a treasure for the few and a mystery to the many. That is why Jesus taught secretly and spoke in strange parables, Mark explained. The other gospel writers did not share this view.

Friday's reading describes the calming of the sea. This brief account is very symbolic. The roaring and heaving seas were calmed and separated by God at creation. The power of God to separate the land from the sea was a sign of his creative power in the face of chaos. Psalm 74:12-14 describes that great act of creation poetically. Psalm 65:7 speaks of the power of God to act upon the storm at sea to bring calm to creation and humanity. Jesus is the embodiment of God's power. He comes to bring calm out of chaos and fear, and a new creation happens in his presence.

The strange story of the Gerasene demoniac comes on Saturday. This story needs to be read with the poet's eye as well as with the historian's interest. Jesus came to drive out the chaos and disorder in the man's life, just as he had stilled the chaos of the water. The death of the pigs may be shocking to the modern reader, but the story would have provided humor to a people who considered swine unclean.

The week of 3 Epiphany

The Old Testament readings:

As we read Second Isaiah, the exile is about to end. We are on the other side of Judah's punishment. God has now cast off Babylonia. They boasted of their victories once too often. They assumed that they would reign supreme forever, never acknowledging that it was by God's will alone that they prospered. God would soon bring them to utter defeat.

On Friday of the week of 1 Epiphany we came to the first of the four "Servant Songs" of Second Isaiah. Each of the songs describes one who is a servant of God called to share in God's creative act of salvation. Though the servant is sometimes referred to in the singular, the writers of Hebrew Scripture often spoke of Israel as a single person. "Jacob, I have called you forth as my chosen one," is a poetic way of referring to the entire nation. And so in Wednesday's text we hear again of Israel's servant role, a role that includes being a light to all of the nations of the world.

The second half of Wednesday's reading describes in poetic terms the return of the people from exile to their homeland. The writer of the Book of Revelation echoed Second Isaiah's words as he described the day of God's final victory: "They shall hunger no more, neither thirst any more; the sun shall not strike them, nor any scorching heat. For the Lamb in the midst of the throne will be their shepherd, and he will guide them to springs of living water; and God will wipe away every tear from their eyes." (Rev. 7:16-17).

The whole created order will rejoice to see Israel return home, and the people themselves will be amazed at how they have grown in number even in exile. (Isaiah 49:20-21). On Friday we hear further poetic descriptions of what it means to be God's servant. There will be times when the servant will be rejected and despised, but the servant must not turn back. Strength will come to the servant with the realization that God will bring final vindication.

The Epistle readings:

Paul traveled through the province of Galatia on his first and second missionary journeys, a territory now part of Turkey, north of the island of Cyprus. He preached a gospel that was free of the restrictions of the Old Testament law. Circumcision of males was not necessary, he proclaimed, nor were the intricate dietary laws of Judaism. None of those ritual practices that had grown up over the generations could bring salvation. The only thing that would bring salvation was faith in the risen Christ. The gift of life in Christ was a free gift, an act of grace that could not be earned, only appreciated.

This was the hope-filled message Paul had taken to the people of the province of Galatia, to the cities of Derbe, Iconium, and Lystra. Read chapter 14 of the Book of the Acts of the Apostles for details of Paul's adventures in that province. Gentiles and some Jews were converted to the Gospel.

Now it is about 54 A.D., and Paul may be in the city of Ephesus. Much to his utter frustration, he has heard that the people of Galatia have accepted a different gospel than Paul's. A "circumcision party" has arrived on the scene, claiming that Paul's gospel of freedom from the strictures of Jewish Law was not correct. To be a Christian, they claim, one must also be a Jew.

This is the background for the reading of Paul's letter to the Galatians. It is an angry letter. We feel Paul's hurt and frustration, along with his determination to reestablish his authority as an apostle who brought the true Gospel to the people.

Paul does not waste any time getting into the argument. On Monday, he moves right in to establish his authority, an authority that exists independently of the apostles in Jerusalem. His experience of the resurrection on the road to Damascus has an authority of its own.

In the text assigned for Tuesday, Paul writes about an agreement with the apostles in Jerusalem. They would honor his missionary work among the gentiles, while Cephas (another name for Peter) would concentrate on Jewish converts. The gentile Christians are not to be forced to accept the Jewish ritual law that includes circumcision and strict dietary practices. Jewish

Christians are to accept gentile Christians as brothers and sisters in Christ. Cephas obviously went back on the agreement.

If we think that the primitive church lived in peace and tranquility, our eyes are quickly opened with this chapter from Galatians. Obviously, Peter and Paul had strong words right in front of the people.

Galatians 2:17-18, included in the Wednesday lection, is a little hazy. Paul's point is that if we are to believe that the Christians' reliance for salvation on Jesus alone, rather than on the codes of Torah, was a cause of their falling into sin, then it would follow that Jesus had caused them to sin. That is absurd! And if Paul were to go back to acceptance of the Law as a way of salvation, then he would be acknowledging that he had been teaching the wrong thing to the gentiles. That, too, is absurd.

The New English Bible translation for Galatians 3:1 begins: "You stupid Galatians. . ." Can you picture the people of Galatia reading this letter for the first time? Paul is angry, and he leaves no doubt about his anger. The point he is making in this chapter is that Abraham was justified, or made righteous, by God because he had faith. Faith is all he had. Only later did the covenant, or Law, made with Moses on Mt. Sinai, come along, but that did not cancel out the original agreement with Abraham.

It was the sinfulness of Abraham's earlier descendants that forced God to lay down a Law, so that the people could see more clearly their transgressions. But since no one could keep the Law perfectly, no one could be made righteous through their vain attempts to follow it.

As a matter of fact, Paul goes on to explain, the Law really levels a curse against everyone who attempts to follow it, since in the Book of Deuteronomy it clearly states that those who do not "abide by all things written in the book of the law. . ." will be cursed. (Gal. 3:10). Well, Jesus deliberately entered into the curse of the Law when he allowed himself to be "hung on a tree." Deuteronomy specified that a man put to death for a crime was to be hung on a tree until sunset as a sign that he was cursed. (Deut. 21:22-23). Jesus, who was hung on the cross was the righteous son of God, proof positive that the Law was impotent or meaningless. The mere hanging on the tree did not make the blessed one cursed. That's proof that the Law bears no weight in the new covenant made through Christ.

Saturday's reading closes our week with the beautiful words, "There is neither Jew nor Greek, there is neither male nor female; for you are all one in Christ Jesus." (Gal. 3:28)

The Gospel readings:

As our new week in Mark begins we are told that Jesus has power over sickness and death. As the woman touches Jesus' cloak she is cured. With a word and a touch Jesus brings the synagogue president's daughter to life.

After words and acts of instruction, Jesus sends his disciples out to proclaim the coming kingdom. They've witnesed the power in their own lives. They've been instructed through parable and vivid experience into the meaning of that coming kingdom. Now it is their turn to act in Jesus' name.

The death of John the Baptist colors our midweek reading with a grim and foreboding feeling. John dies for standing for the word and truth of God in the face of evil. His ministry is rejected by the authority, and he dies an unjust death. John's death points ahead to Jesus' death.

The familiar story of the feeding of the 5,000 is the appointed lesson for Thursday. One of the beautiful images of the coming kingdom, or reign, of God prevalent in Jesus' time was the messianic banquet. This feeding incident on the hillside can be seen as a foretaste of that banquet. Notice the Eucharistic-like words and actions in the description of Jesus taking the bread, breaking and blessing it, and then distributing it to the assembled people. Jesus comes to gather the family of God. Like the father of the Jewish home or the religious leader of a group of Jewish men, he blesses, breaks, and distributes the bread in table fellowship as an expression of the people's relationship to the living God.

Feeding stories were not unique to Jesus. See 2 Kings 4:42-44 for a similar story told about the great prophet Elisha. People in Jesus' time would have made a connection.

The calming and healing motif is followed in Friday's reading. Jesus is seen walking on water. He is about to pass the disciples by when he notices their fear and exercises power over the elements. He walks over the waters that represent death and chaos to ancient peoples. Some scholars feel that this event may have actually been a resurrection appearance. No matter; God is in charge in this life as well as in the next. Even as the waters threaten to close over our heads, Christ walks with us.

Think about St. Paul's controversy with the Jewish authorities as you read Saturday's lesson. Paul's insistence that gentiles could enter into relationship with Christ without following the strict dietary rituals of the orthodox Jew is given the authority of Jesus in these passages. It is not what goes into us that stands between us and holiness. It is what comes out of our lives that is important. We dare not substitute empty ritual for life-giving service to God in our lives. Realize the radical nature of these words as you read them. The ancient practices followed by generations of faithful Jews are questioned.

The week of 4 Epiphany

The Old Testament readings:

Israel must have a sharp memory, Second Isaiah tells the people, for it is in remembering how God acted powerfully in the past that we will have the courage to see that God is about to act again. The new act of creation is about to happen. Rahab, referred to in Sunday's reading, was a mythic sea monster. To defeat Rahab was a way of saying that God had defeated the forces of chaos. The name was sometimes sarcastically applied to Egypt.

Israel is depicted as a woman mourning the death of all of her sons and devastated with terrible tragedies. There is none to raise this woman up, and yet she is beckoned to rise for God will take away from her the cup of wrath that she has been forced to drink. From now on those who tormented this woman (Jerusalem) will have to drink from the cup of torment themselves. Babylonia take note!

Tuesday's reading begins on the same note as Monday's reading. Jerusalem is to rise up to a new day! The prophet's poetic imagery lifts us to the watchmen's towers in verse 8. "How beautiful upon the mountains are the feet of him who brings glad tidings. . ." (Isaiah 52:7). The watchman shouts to the people in the streets: "God is your king! God brings victory at last!"

We do not read the fourth of the great Servant Songs, Isaiah 52:13-53:12, this week. Our reading of that beautiful passage is reserved for Holy Week where it is assigned to be read at the Eucharist on Palm Sunday and again on Good Friday. You may want to include the passage in your reading this week so that you see it in the context of Second Isaiah's other writings.

In the film and play, "Fiddler on the Roof," Tevye cries out to God at one point saying, "God we are your chosen people. Why don't you choose someone else for awhile!" He speaks out of the generations of oppression and suffering that his people have known.

The followers of Jesus saw the significance of Second Isaiah's Suffering Servant songs in a whole new light. Jesus was that servant.

To appreciate the significance of Thursday's reading, take a moment and read Isaiah 25:6-8, a description of the messianic banquet of God. This rich imagery is picked up in the closing words of Second Isaiah. He promises that nations will come streaming to the table where Israel is already seated.

Canticle 10 assigned for reading at Morning Prayer (BCP, pp. 86-87) is a part of our text assigned for Thursday. God's word is a power that creates. Nothing can defeat it. God's way and thought are as far above ours as the heavens are above the earth.

We move on Friday to the writings of Third Isaiah. Life back in Judah after the return of the exiles was not easy. People quickly became disillusioned when their dreams of restoration as a great nation were not realized. Third Isaiah wrote to encourage them and to confront them with their unfaithfulness.

Judah must not forget to do justice as called for in the Torah. This is the opening theme set by Third Isaiah. The universal salvation expressed to the exiles by Second Isaiah is continued. No one, not even the rejected eunuchs, will be excluded from God's salvation. (It was a eunuch who was baptized by Philip as he accepted the salvation of God revealed in Christ, we are told in the eighth chapter of Acts.) Jesus quoted from Third Isaiah as he drove out the money changers from the Temple: "For my house shall be called a house of prayer for all peoples."

Third Isaiah echoes the earlier pre-exilic prophets as he warns the returning people against drifting from their pure worship of God.

The Epistle reading:
Circumcision was anathema to Paul, for it meant that the Christian had no faith in the free grace of Christ. How could the Christians possibly fall for the Judaizers' line when they had accepted Paul's gospel of freedom with such enthusiasm only a short time before?

More personal details about Paul come in Tuesday's reading. Apparently he was sick when he first arrived in Galatia. It was his sickness that opened doors to him among the people so that he could preach and minister to them. Paul uses a story from the Book of Genesis to form an allegory of life under the "gospel" of the Judaizers and life under the gospel Paul preached. Abraham's first son was born to his slave, Hagar, who was later driven out into the wilderness. Hagar represents the covenant made with Moses at Mt. Sinai. The son born to Sarah is the son of promise, Isaac. The new covenant people are related to Isaac.

Paul's anger leads to some strong statements. Thursday's reading closes with the admonition, "I wish those who unsettle you would mutilate themselves!" (Gal.5:12, RSV). The New English Bible is more blunt in translating the Greek: "As for those agitators, they had better go the whole way and make eunuchs of themselves!" Paul does not mince words!

Beginning with Galatians 5:13, we move into a section devoted to Paul's words about what life under the freedom of the Gospel is to look like. The question, "What are we going to do as a result of our freedom?" is the focal point of his writing at this point. His words of direction even include an admonition to pay their Christian teacher who is sharing the Gospel with them. Paul points to the authenticity of his letter. He closes it with his own hand and writes so that everyone can see his "large letters." Paul often dictated his letters to a scribe.

The Gospel readings:

Notice the exhaustion of Jesus as you begin this week's reading. A gentile woman places a demand on him for healing. Jesus' blunt words to her may shock us as we read them today: "Let the children first be fed, for it is not right to take the children's bread and throw it to the dogs." (Mark 7:27). The tone of Jesus' voice and the expression on his face are not seen nor heard by us, but in any case, the woman throws his words back to him. Perhaps amused at her quickness, he responds to her request.

Ironically, it is a woman considered by some "unfit to receive the children's bread" who shows the faith in Jesus that "the children" themselves lack. Perhaps it is the irony of this acceptance-in-contrast-to-rejection that causes Jesus to speak to the woman, using an expression of disdain common in his time.

One healing is quickly followed by another, as the deaf and mute man comes to him. In contrast to the "dumb" people unable and unwilling to proclaim the new age that has dawned with Jesus, this "dumb" man now speaks. Isaiah's words come true: "On that day the deaf shall hear the words of a book, and out of their gloom and darkness the eyes of the blind shall see." (Isaiah 29:18)

You are not seeing double as you study Saturday's lesson. Last week we read that Jesus fed 5,000 people, and now we read that Jesus feeds 4,000 people, in a very similar account. Many scholars feel that this is simply a "doublet," or a repeating of the same story by Mark.

The Pharisees demand a sign from Jesus, who denies that God will send signs "in this generation." The disciples, however, had been seeing signs all around them as they follow Jesus, especially in the miracles of the loaves! Despite the signs, they remain blind to the significance of Jesus' life among them. The reference to yeast, or heaven, found in the reading, was a common metaphor of the day. Evil rises up in life, infecting all of society, just as yeast rises up in dough. (This explains why yeast, a metaphor for evil, is removed from Jewish households at the time of Passover to this day.)

We then read of the healing of the blind man at Bethsaida. The blind man can now see far more clearly than those blind disciples! Real sight begins to come to Peter, however, as he realizes who Jesus is, but he still cannot see as God would have him see. He cannot see that to be Messiah means that Jesus must suffer and die.

This passage marks the hinge point of the Gospel of Mark. From this point on Jesus moves toward Jerusalem and the passion.

The collect for Friday, on page 99 of the Book of Common Prayer, sets the theme for Thursday's reading: "Almighty God, whose most dear Son went not up to joy but first he suffered pain, and entered not into glory before he was crucified; Mercifully grant that we, walking in the way of the cross, may find it none other than the way of life and peace." The disciples of Jesus must bear the cross in every age. These words stand in stark contrast to the assumption that when one follows Jesus, life will be peaceful and profitable.

On Friday you may want to refer to Exodus 24:1-18 for background to appreciate the significance of the transfiguration. Jesus takes his disciples "up to the mountain" for a revelation of the new Law, which is Jesus, a Law not written on stone, but written on the hearts of the people. (See Jeremiah 31:31). It was Moses who went "up into the mountain" to receive the tablets of the covenant on Mt. Sinai.

Several other points need to be kept in mind: Elijah was the great prophet of Israel who lived in the time of King Ahab and Queen Jezebel. (1 Kings). Tradition held that Elijah would return at the coming of the Messiah to herald in the day of the Lord. The Feast of Booths was a joyous fall harvest festival in which shelters were erected from harvest stalks and vines to celebrate God's presence with the people as they wandered in the wilderness. According to Zechariah 14:16-19, all nations would celebrate that feast together at the coming of the final day of the Lord. Peter's mention of the tent (booth, or tabernacle), is a reference to that great expectation.

Tradition held that Elijah's role at the ushering in of the day of the Lord was to purify the people of God, to turn them back to Torah. Jesus saw this as the role of John the Baptist, who had already come and been killed by Herod.

When Moses came down from the mountain after receiving the tablets of the Law, he was immediately met with confusion and loss of faith on the part of the people. (Exodus 32). In his absence, they had created a golden calf to worship. Now as Jesus comes down from the Mountain of Revelation, he also meets with the loss of faith and confusion among his disciples.

The week of 5 Epiphany

The Old Testament readings:

The words of anger and condemnation directed against Judah become words of hope and comfort as we resume our reading of Third Isaiah this week. God cannot be angry at men and women forever, for the very breath of God was placed within them. (Genesis 2:7). Moreover, God calls new people into covenant relationship: "Peace, peace, to the far and to the near, says the Lord." (Isaiah 57:19).

Monday's reading questions the empty ritual practices of the people. True worship of God is to have compassion for the poor and struggling. True worship is to do justice. These words are a vivid reminder to us that our liturgy shared together in the parish must be lived out in our lives or else we, too, stand condemned. Third Isaiah's words echo the concerns of Amos: "I hate, I despise your feasts, and I take no delight in your solemn assemblies...But let justice roll down like waters, and righteousness like an everflowing stream." (Amos 5:21, 24).

God puts on the battle gear of integrity, salvation and vengeance as he carries out mighty acts of historic significance. The writer of the Epistle to the Ephesians picked up Third Isaiah's imagery when he urged the Christians to put on the armor of God. Paul himself used the image of putting on the armor of God in his first letter to the Thessalonians. (Ephesians 6:14-16, 1 Thessalonians 5:8). God's spirit placed in the minds and mouths of the people will never fail. Christians see pentecostal significance to these words. We are inspired (in-spirited) by the Holy Spirit to share in God's creative purpose in the world.

An Epiphany theme is set in Thursday's reading. All nations shall stream to God: "A multitude of camels shall cover you, the young camels of Midian and Ephah; all those from Sheba shall come." (Isaiah 60:7). The glory of God revealed to Isreal at Sinai will be a glory revealed to all nations in the coming time. Portions of this day's reading are found in Canticle 11, "The Third Song of Isaiah" appointed for Morning Prayer. (BCP, 87).

When Jesus opened the scroll in his hometown synagogue he chose the words we read on Friday: "The Spirit of the Lord God is upon me, because the Lord has anointed me to bring good tidings (good news, gospel) to the afflicted; he has sent me to bind up the broken hearted, to proclaim liberty to the captives, and the opening of the prison to those who are bound. . ." (Isaiah 61:1). He knew the impact it would have on the people as he added his own commentary following his reading: "Today this scripture has been fulfilled in your hearing." (Luke 4:21)

In this coming age, Judah will be given a new name. She will be recognized as the bride of God and honored among all nations. God will delight in her as a bridegroom delights in his bride. On this note of hope to a despairing people we end our week in Third Isaiah.

The Epistle readings:

Our readings of Galatians is concluded on Monday. We spend the balance of this week in the Second Letter of Paul to Timothy, one of the three pastoral epistles, so called because each deals with the pastoral concerns of the primitive church. Many scholars feel that though these epistles are attributed to Paul, in fact they were written by disciples of Paul at a later date. Other scholars think the pastorals are, indeed, from the hand of Paul himself, written at the time of his imprisonment in Ephesus or Rome. (Second Timothy purports to have been written from Rome.)

Suspicion about Paul's authorship stems from the concerns of the pastoral epistles. Paul lived with the expectation that Christ would return very soon to begin the reign of God. The pastoral epistles, on the other hand, seem to have been written at a time when Christians were beginning to realize that they had to be ready for the long haul in the present age.

Read Acts 16:1-5 to learn of Timothy's place in Paul's ministry.

Note on Tuesday the reference to "sound words" and the need to ". . .guard the truth that has been entrusted to you. . ." (2 Timothy 1:13-14). Faith and truth are now equated with a specific doctrine that must be treasured and guarded against the heresies of the time.

An ancient hymn may lie embedded in Wednesday's reading: "If we have died with him, we shall also live with him; if we endure we shall also reign with him..." (2 Timothy 2:11-13). Paul's own struggles were perceived by him as a part of the suffering that would lead to the victory of Christ's resurrection. Suffering is not empty and meaningless. In Christ it is life-giving as one identifies personally with the suffering of Christ.

Notice on Friday the emphasis on the importance of scripture in equipping the Christian "for every good work." (2 Timothy 3:17). These words remind us of the role of scripture in our lives. We read so that we may be properly equipped for every good work.

The Gospel readings:

The Gospel of Mark is addressed to a church under persecution. The converts have been promised eternal life in the risen Christ, but they are now experiencing martyrdom, ridicule, rejection and suffering. The gospel, starting with Mark 8:34 and continuing through the end of chapter 10, is for new converts and for the church in general. "This is what it means to be a follower of the risen Christ," Mark is saying.

Tuesday's reading sparks strong words for the church. The "little ones," or recent converts, must not be tempted to forego the Gospel for the sake of present comfort. To tempt the weak is to invite instant condemnation for yourself. Temptation to sin must be resisted at all costs. A person's hand might reach out to sin, the foot might be the part of the body that would direct one to leave the path of the Gospel, the eye might see the opportunity to sin. "Cut them out," if need be, to avoid the sin. The closing words for Monday warn the Christian that being tested by "salt and fire" is part of what life-in-Christ means. The Christian is to "salt," or flavor the environment. Tasteless salt is worthless.

Marriage and divorce within the Christian covenant is the focus for Wednesday's readings. Jesus' words seem restrictive in our age when divorce is recognized by the church. Remember that in Jesus' time, wives could be easily divorced by their husbands and had very few rights of their own. Jesus' teaching on divorce protected the woman and affirmed her status in her husband's house. Historically, the church has exercised the privilege of modifying Jesus' teaching in the light of the guidance of the Holy Spirit. Matthew 18:18 has been seen as the authority for this interpretive aspect of the church's life: "Truly, I say to you, whatever you bind on earth shall be bound in heaven, and whatever you loose on earth shall be loosed in heaven."

Jesus' words to be read on Thursday are harsh. It is impossible for the rich and powerful to enter into the kingdom of God. We try to modify those words and set them aside in our affluent culture, but Jesus saw clearly that it was the poor and powerless who responded to his words, his healings and his presence. There is a complete reversal of life when God's reign comes. The "first shall be last and the last shall be first" is a common theme throughout Christian scripture.

Discipleship also results in a reversal of expectations, we learn on Friday. James and John expect reward and prestige. Instead, they will receive the cup and baptism of the martyrdom. One who is a disciple is one who serves, rather than one who is served. Think of the impact of those words on a church suffering from persecution. Think of the impact of the words on the church in Poland, Central America, South Africa and other places where Christians suffer for their faith and their convictions. These are the people who truly know the sense and urgency of the reign of God. Jesus' words about affluence come home to us.

Each day in our reading we move closer to Jerusalem. Saturday's walk with Christ brings us to Jericho, 12 hard, uphill hours from the great city. Through faith, Bartimaeus, whom Jesus meets outside of Jericho, receives his sight. Bartimaeus' sight stands in contrast to the blindness of the Pharisees and Sadducees and, indeed, to the blindness of the disciples themselves!

The week of 6 Epiphany

The Old Testament readings:

On Tuesday and Wednesday we read a psalm written by Third Isaiah as an entreaty to God. He pleads the people's cause before God. The Lord has redeemed the people in the past. Why does God not "come down" now and shake the heart of the nation so that alien peoples can know the mighty power of the God of Israel?

Thursday's and Friday's readings seem to be an answer to the psalmist's plea. God has seen the people totally reject the covenant. They have broken every commandment even to the eating of swine flesh. Surely they have earned God's judgment. Still, despite the evil ways of the people, a remnant shall be saved for a new day with God. The whole nation will not be destroyed. The primitive church saw the promise of a restored remnant as applying to the followers of Jesus.

There is hope at the last, the prophet says. God will create "new heavens and a new earth." (Isaiah 65:17). A perfect reign of justice and peace shall come. Long life will be the gift. Even the wolf and the lamb will feed together. The "holy mountain" mentioned in the text is Jerusalem, the sacred city.

Saturday's and Sunday's readings continue in a hopeful vein. "Heaven is my throne and the earth is my footstool . . ." (Isaiah 66:1) The empty formalism of temple practice must not replace a "humble and contrite" spirit. (Isaiah 66:2). Empty rites must not replace the awareness of the downtrodden. It is the humble and the oppressed whom God is concerned about, not the intricacies of temple cultus. Peace will come like an overflowing river. As you read Isaiah 66:13 on Sunday notice the strong female imagery associated with God: "As one whom his mother comforts, so I will comfort you."

The Epistle readings:

The familiar saying, "Christ Jesus came into the world to save sinners," (1 Timothy 1:15) is seen in its biblical context on

Monday. Paul, or the disciple of Paul, was obviously quoting a saying in circulation within the church. It could have been a creedal statement or a fragment of a hymn. Tuesday's reading, 1 Timothy 1:18-2:8, includes directives for the gathered church at prayer that still guide us as we share the Prayers of the People at the Holy Eucharist. On Wednesday qualifications for bishops and deacons are given in 1 Timothy 3:1-16. Note that only two orders of ordained ministers are listed in this passage.

In 1 Timothy 5:19, assigned for Friday, we come across the Greek word, *presbyteros,* translated "elder." John Calvin and John Wesley saw this as evidence that elders and bishops were terms used interchangeably in the primitive church. They claimed that *episkopos* (the Greek word we translate as "bishop") and *presbyteros,* were really one order of ordained ministry. It was on this authority that John Wesley ordained two men as *presbyteros,* or elders, and sent them to the mission field in America. Since Wesley had been ordained in the Church of England as a *presbyteros* he reasoned that he had the authority to ordain others. Most Christian bodies, including the Episcopal Church, hold that there are three distinct orders of ordained ministry—deacon, priest and bishop.

Watch for another ancient Christian hymn in 1 Timothy 3:16: "He was manifested in the flesh, vindicated in the Spirit..." We can say that the first hymnal of the church was the New Testament itself, enriched by a tradition of hymns and canticles, with texts from the Old Testament as well as the New Testament. It is too bad that we don't have the tunes that went with those early Christian hymns!

"For the love of money is the root of all evils..." (1 Timothy 6:10). Sound familiar? Well, here is the origin of that saying.

The Gospel readings:

We move out of the teaching, or catechetical, section of Mark's Gospel as we begin our reading Monday. In order to appreciate the traditional Palm Sunday passage, you need to keep a few facts in mind: The horse was a beast of war and conquest.

When a king came on an ass, it meant he came to announce a reign of peace and justice. The spreading of garments and branches on the ground was an ancient sign of greeting to the king. (See 2 Kings 9:13.) At the great Jewish festival of Tabernacles (also called the Feast of Booths) and again at the time of Hannukah, branches were waved and words from Psalm 118:25-26 were shouted by the people. Hannukah celebrated the rededication of the temple by the Jews at the time the Greeks were driven out in 164 B.C. Tabernacles was celebrated as an annual renewal of the covenant between God and the nation. It was also a time of recalling the years of wilderness pilgrimage in which God led them toward the Promised Land.

One of the images of the coming reign of God was that all nations would join the Jews in Jerusalem for the great Feast of Tabernacles. (See Zechariah 14:16-21.)

Incidentally, "Hosanna" meant "Save now!" in Hebrew.

As we reflect on the ancient traditions associated with Jesus' entry into Jerusalem, we can see both the political and religious impact of his action. In a sense, Jesus was acting out of a living parable of his life and death among the people. He might have said, "I come to rededicate the Temple, to announce the dawn of the reign of God. I come as the Prince of Peace."

On Tuesday we read the events associated with Monday of what we call Holy Week. It is now the "next day" after the triumphal entry, and Jesus again enters the city after spending the night at Bethany, a town about 1¾ miles from Jerusalem.

The curse of the fig tree can best be understood as a parable told by Jesus (see Luke 13:6-9) that the writer of Mark placed in the narrative to emphasize the point of what was happening in these final days.

A little background is necessary to appreciate the cleansing of the Temple scene. Jesus was not upset with the money-changing and selling going on in the Temple. That was essential for the carrying on of the rites of the Temple. It was the unfair practices that had grown up around the money-changing and sale of sacrificial animals that aroused his anger. But of more importance, Jesus was acting out a prophetic drama to make a clear statement to the people that he was announcing the inauguration of the messianic age. Take a moment now and read Jeremiah 7:1-16, Isaiah 56:7, and Malachi 3:3-5 so you can see Jesus' activity here through the same perspective as the people of his time. You may also want to read Jeremiah 13:1-11 and Isaiah 20:1-6 for examples of similar dramatic actions by the prophets.

Jesus' actions at the Temple were not lost on the authorities. They moved quickly to entrap him, discredit him, and bring him before the Jewish and Roman courts.

Thursday's reference to paying taxes is not meant to imply that there are two separate realms of responsibility in the world, the sacred and the secular. The "things that are God's" are everything in heaven and earth, if we take the Torah seriously. The closing words on Thursday are subtle. (Mark 12:26-27). If God identified himself to Moses at the burning bush as "I *am* the God of Abraham" rather than "I *was* the God of Abraham," surely that indicated that Abraham still had a living relationship with God.

Friday you will read words familiar from the Book of Common Prayer: "Hear, O Israel: The Lord our God, the Lord is one..." Note that these are not Jesus' own words; he quotes from the Torah (first five books of Hebrew Scripture), from Deuteronomy 6:4-5 and Leviticus 19:18.

The opening words on Saturday (Mark 12:35-36) can be confusing as Jesus is again making subtle use of scripture to prove his point. It was thought by many Jews that the Messiah would be a military hero who would reestablish Israel as a major power. (See Jeremiah 23:5-6, Amos 9:11-12, Ezekiel 37:23-24, and Daniel 9:25-26.) This Messiah would be a descendant of David. Psalm 110, attributed to King David, reads in verse 1, "The Lord says to my lord: 'Sit at my right hand, till I make your enemies your footstool.'" The psalm had taken on messianic meaning in the time of Jesus. Lord was seen as referring to the coming Messiah. *If* David wrote the psalm, Jesus was saying, then how can he call the Messiah, Lord, and at the same time be the father of the Messiah? The Messiah was to be more than a military hero, more than a descendant of David. "Enlarge your vision of the Messiah," Jesus was saying.

The week of 7 Epiphany

The Old Testament readings:

The Book of Ruth is a charming story of King David's great-grandmother whose commitment to her mother-in-law, Naomi, serves as a model of devotion for succeeding generations.

If a man had no male heirs it was like being condemned to extinction. Eternal life was not a part of the understanding of the Israelites. Life was carried on in one's sons. When Elimelech and his two sons died leaving three widows, an entire family was condemned to extinction.

To preserve the male line, brothers and male relatives had the obligation to marry a widow with the hope that a son would be born through the marriage. Property, also, depended upon the male relatives for restoration. Naomi had a small piece of property in Israel, but it would take a male relative to redeem it for her. A quick reading of Leviticus 25:25 and Deuteronomy 25:5-10 will provide you with scriptural reference points for the Book of Ruth.

Ruth took a risk as she decided to go with her mother-in-law. She could expect no rights in Israel. Women were simply considered a man's property. A widow was helpless. Thus, Ruth moved out in faith much as Abraham and Sarah had.

The Book of Ruth may have been written during the reign of David or Solomon as a means of providing added authenticity for David and his line of male heirs on the throne. Some scholars, however, think the book was written after the Babylonian exile during a time when foreign wives were being rejected because it was felt that they were evil in the sight of God. Ruth provided a strong counterbalance to such exclusive fundamentalist tendencies. King David's great-grandmother was, after all, a foreigner herself!

You may recognize familiar words in Tuesday's reading: "...for where you go I will go, and where you lodge I will lodge..." (Ruth 1:16) The liturgical greeting, "the Lord be with you," will also be a familiar phrase read on Wednesday, a reminder that our liturgical traditions have deep roots.

Ruth gleans in the fields of Boaz. At harvest time some of the crops had to be left in the field for the poor to harvest for themselves. (See Deut. 24:19-22 and Lev. 19:9-10.)

In Thursday's reading, Naomi realizes that Boaz offers the opportunity to exercise the next-of-kin rights. She "primes the pump" a bit with her instructions to Ruth about meeting Boaz on his threshing floor. The actions of Ruth and Boaz that you will read about on Friday symbolize an offer and acceptance of marriage. Your imagination may lead you to think of more than a symbolic encounter between them. Certainly there is a seductive quality about Ruth's visit, but the purpose of her action was to institute a marriage that would assure the family line of Boaz' next of kin.

Interesting legal customs of ancient Israel become evident for us in Friday's reading. Boaz waits at the town gate for the other eligible relatives to come along and for 10 men who could render judgment in the case. The town gate was the courthouse for each community and a quorum of 10 men served as judges in legal cases. The other male relative was interested in the property rights but not the marriage rights, thus leaving the way open for Boaz both to marry Ruth and reclaim the piece of land. Boaz, Ruth and Naomi seem to "live happily ever after" as our story ends. The last four verses of the book, not assigned in the reading, point from Boaz and Ruth to King David.

The Epistle readings:

Paul's Second Letter to the Corinthians will be our focus for the next three weeks. In this letter we see Paul struggling with issues that were dividing the church in Corinth. We sense his pain, his anger, his love for the people, and most of all his vision of what it means to be given a new life in Christ. Conflict is nothing new to the church, we discover as we read this epistle. Conflict has been a part of the church since the earliest times. With the exception of the Epistle to the Romans, all of Paul's letters were written into situations of conflict and disagreement.

Apparently the church in Corinth had split when several strong persons in the church disagreed with Paul's theological ideas and raised doubts about his authority to preach the Gospel in the first place. A visit from Paul to heal the division ended in disaster. The division of the church only deepened. Paul wrote an angry letter back to the church a short time after he left Corinth. That letter resulted in disciplinary action against the troublemakers and a restoration of unity. What we have in Second Corinthians is a follow-up letter in which Paul rejoices at the new harmony, but continues to stress his authority and credentials as an apostle.

The letter opens with a discussion of suffering. Suffering took on meaning for Paul because he saw it as a personal way of participating in the redeeming work of Christ. What he went through for the Gospel was his self-offering, a way of participating in the healing act of Christ made known on the cross. (With Paul's words in mind, my aunt offered the pain she suffered from cancer as her living sacrifice to Christ, a way of participating in the healing power of the cross herself.)

The reference to Paul's strife in Asia remains a mystery for there is no historic or scriptural record of what happened to him there.

Wednesday's reading reveals the anguish Paul experienced as he related to the Corinthian church. He felt so badly that he had been a part of the pain felt by the people.

Having expressed his feelings, Paul could turn to matters of theology. The glory known in Christ is far beyond the momentary glory experienced by Moses when he received the covenant. The Torah placed a barrier between God and people. Though Torah pointed out the way of righteousness, no one could walk in that way. In Christ, the barrier had been removed. It was as if a veil was lifted and one could see God face to face at last. One living in union with Christ reflects Christ's glory and is transfigured into the likeness of Christ as the relationship deepens.

Watch for familiar quotations as you follow the lectionary readings on Friday and Saturday.

The Gospel readings:

For the next two weeks we read the Sermon on the Mount from the Gospel of Matthew. These lectionary texts assigned for the late weeks of Epiphany are read only in those years when Easter and Lent fall late on the calendar. Thus the readings do not always fit with those of the weeks preceding and following them. These are "bonus texts."

The Sermon on the Mount is not really a sermon. The writer of the Gospel of Matthew had an extensive collection of Jesus' sayings that people remembered and repeated orally for a generation. Matthew collected these sayings and placed them in the context of new commandments given by Jesus to his disciples on the "mountain." The Jewish Christians who heard them would immediately think of the commandments Moses gave Israel "on the mountain" at Sinai. Matthew was making the point that Jesus was the new Moses for Israel. Indeed, the followers of Jesus are the new Israel. This is a new covenant made with a new nation. The writer of the Gospel of Luke followed a similar pattern, except that his collection of sayings was given to the disciples on a plain. (See Luke 6:17-49.)

The Beatitudes as stated in the Gospel of Luke (See Luke 6:20-25) are radical statements of reversal. Those who are fat and happy in the present age will find their fortunes reversed in the age to come. Those who struggle and suffer in the present age will find their reward when the reign of God fully dawns. Refer also to the Song of Mary, Luke 1:47-55, for another example of the reversal theme in Luke. There are no woes to the rich and the powerful in Matthew's account, and "the poor" who are blessed become "the poor *in spirit*" with Matthew's sermon. In either case, Jesus' promise is clear. Those who struggle for righteousness and the Gospel are blessed in the sight of God and they shall be comforted.

For those who think that Jesus came to overthrow the Law, his words read Tuesday are a quick corrective. Jesus came not to abolish the Law of the Torah but to fulfill it. The 613 commandments of the Torah set forth guidelines for the faithful Jews covering every aspect of their lives. The ultimate purpose of life for the Jew was to know and to follow the Torah. The commandments were not great burdens to the Jew. They were constant reminders to them of their covenant with God who guided every waking and sleeping moment. But the commandments of the Law, Jesus would say, were only the top layer of righteousness. One had to go to the heart of the intent of the Torah commandments truly to respond to God's covenant.

For example, anger is the seedbed for murder. Even to feel anger for another mens that one has stepped outside God's intention for man and woman. Loving one's neighbor, as Torah commands, is only the beginning of what it means to love. We must learn to love our enemy, as well as our neighbor. Jesus' words on the Law speak of a new ethic, a new response that is called for as the kingdom of heaven breaks into the present order. This ethic of the reign of heaven makes little sense in terms of the ethic of the present age, but God calls us to live as if the reign of heaven has already fully come.

Notice the admonition in Matthew 5:23-24 that we must make peace before going to the altar. We are called in the liturgy of the Holy Eucharist to pass the peace. It is not just a simple greeting between people. It is a vivid reminder of Jesus' words.

The restrictions on divorce that Jesus promulgated need to be read in the light of divorce customs of the time. Under some rabbinic interpretations, a man could divorce his wife with a mere statement of intent. The wife had few protections. Jesus' words gave women some rights. Marriage was not to be taken lightly.

Saturday's admonition on prayer is not meant to denounce all forms of public worship. Humility is the key to prayer. One must avoid acts of officious public piety.

The week of 8 Epiphany

The Old Testament readings:

For the next three weeks we will be reading from the Book of Deuteronomy. For the historical setting of the book, take a moment and read 2 Kings 22:3-23:3. King Josiah, one of Judah's last kings before the Babylonian exile, began a major religious reform. The Book of Deuteronomy was the cornerstone of that reform. Supposedly discovered in the Temple during its reconstruction, the book purports to be words spoken by Moses just before his death and the entrance of our biblical ancestors into the Promised Land. In fact, the book appears to have been written in King Josiah's time or a few years earlier. (640-609 B.C.).

Deuteronomy is a part of an extended narrative that provides a summary of Israel's history from the time of Joshua and the taking of Canaan up to the time of Josiah. The Book of Deuteronomy and the historic narrative are written from a distinct viewpoint: when the people of Israel follow the covenant, they prosper from God's blessing; when they break the Covenant, they suffer at the hand of God who raises up enemies and natural disasters to chastise a wayward people.

The need to remember the mighty acts of God in order to remain faithful to the covenant is another recurring theme in Deuteronomy. Remembrance of the past leads to consciousness of God's presence in every generation.

Incidentally, Mt. Horeb is the deuteronomic writer's name for Mt. Sinai.

Tuesday's reading makes reference to Moses' punishment by God: "Furthermore the Lord was angry with me on your account, and he swore that I should not cross the Jordan..." (Deut. 4:21). As background for that statement read Numbers 20:1-12, Deuteronomy 1:19-40, and Deuteronomy 32:48-52. The people's faithless fear of the inhabitants of Canaan and Moses' action in drawing water out of the rock in the wilderness of Zin (or Sin) were perceived as the reasons Moses and the

people were forced to wander in the wilderness for a generation. Why God was perceived as being angry with Moses for
striking the rock is not clear from the text.

The familiar Ten Commandments, or decalogue, is Friday's
reading. Just before the recitation of the commandments, Moses
again rehearses God's mighty acts for Israel. In response to
God's action for Israel, the people are called into a covenant
relationship with God. This writing follows the ancient pattern
of covenant making between a king and a people. The king
would rehearse for the people what he had done for them, and
he would call them into a covenant relationship. At the
Eucharist the priest recalls the mighty acts of God in the prayer
of consecration: "Holy and gracious Father; in your infinite love
you made us for yourself; and, when we had fallen into sin
and become subject to evil and death, you, in your mercy, sent
Jesus Christ. . ." (BCP, p. 362). We then move to the altar for
the sacrament, a means of renewing our covenant with God
through Christ.

Saturday's reading is a grand scene in which Moses recalls
the appearance of God at Mt. Horeb when the covenant was
made. The scene may reflect a liturgical celebration in the
Temple, enacted periodically to renew the covenant. In the days
of the Temple the people would have celebrated the covenant
with incense, processions, and great pageantry.

The Epistle readings:

Prepare for some tough words from Paul this week. He's
angry, hurt, defensive of his authority, and threatening a third
visit to Corinth to straighten out the recalcitrant church. Many
scholars think that the last three chapters of 2 Corinthians are,
in fact, the stern letter that Paul refers to earlier in the epistle.
See if you agree. The theory certainly makes sense. Paul's words
of peace and reconciliation shift in these last chapters to angry
defense of his apostolic authority. The two letters, scholars believe, were simply combined on one scroll with the later letter
preceding the first.

Apparently a group within the Corinthian church (or perhaps people coming into the church after Paul left Corinth) have managed to assume authority. Paul sarcastically calls them the "superlative apostles." They preach a different gospel and ridicule Paul's authority within the church. On the basis of his defense, imagine what was being said about Paul. The superlative apostles have made their impact on the church. Paul felt the message of the Gospel itself was at stake. The battle went beyond issues of personal leadership.

Biting sarcasm is a part of this angry letter. If those superlative apostles are going to boast about their leadership, well let Paul boast too. He proceeds to do so in striking terms, revealing his own struggle to proclaim the Gospel in process.

Note that he acknowledges he is not an eloquent speaker. This passage always reminds me of the story in Acts 20:7-12 about the young man who fell asleep during the long sermon of Paul and fell out the window. The writer of Acts would seem to agree with Paul!

Part of Paul's boasting leads him to tell of intense visions he had in which he lost all sense of physical feeling. Thursday's reading begins with his description of the experience.

No one has been able to define the "thorn in the flesh" that plagued Paul and humbled him. The beautiful words of 2 Corinthians 12:9 are often quoted in Christian literature: "My grace is sufficient for you, for my power is made perfect in weakness."

Paul's sarcasm grows more biting in Friday's reading, and we end our week in 2 Corinthians with a threat, a promise, from Paul to return "in power" to speak with apostolic authority. The letter closes with a doxology familiar from its association with Morning and Evening Prayer: "The grace of the Lord Jesus Christ and the love of God and the fellowship of the Holy Spirit be with you all." (2 Cor. 13:14, BCP, pp. 102, 126).

The Gospel readings:

Jesus' teaching on prayer introduced on Saturday, continues as we begin our new week in Matthew with Jesus' introduction of the Lord's Prayer to the disciples. This prayer is the model prayer for Christians.

Note well the petitions that can lose their impact through familiarity. We pray that the kingdom may come "on earth as it is in heaven." It is the ethic of the kingdom, not the ethic of the world that demands our allegiance. We pray for the bread that will sustain us. We have no right for a wealth of bread, only that which we need for the daily life. Then comes the petition of radical forgiveness. To paraphrase the prayer, "Forgive us to the extent that we are able to forgive others." In Jewish practice one cannot pray for something one is not willing to do. We can only pray for the forgiveness we are willing to give.

The "temptation" or "test" (the more accurate translation) referred to in the Lord's Prayer is the final trial that comes at the end of the age. We pray that we may be spared the anguish of that period of trial and testing. May we be spared from evil, or the "evil one," at that moment and at every moment.

The Lord's Prayer is spoken from the viewpoint of God in the sense that it calls us to pray as God would have us to pray. God sees our need in terms of the need of all humanity. We ourselves, on the other hand, view prayer from our limited perspective in which we seem to be the center of the universe. To pray the Lord's Prayer is to see momentarily through the eyes of God. It is truly the *Lord's* Prayer, and not ours.

Familiar words greet us in Wednesday's reading: ". . .therefore I tell you, do not be anxious about your life. . ." (Matt. 6:25). This call to look at the lilies of the field clothed more beautifully than Solomon in all his splendor is not just a suggestion about an attitude for mental health. To be a part of the coming reign of heaven means a total concentration on responding to God. Alcoholics Anonymous has a saying that guides the lives of its members: "One day at a time." Take the day, live it fully, and trust that the next day will take care of itself.

The Golden Rule is a part of Thursday's reading (Matt. 7:1-12). A potpourri of Jesus' sayings was collected by the writer of the gospel, sayings about prayer, forgiveness, and Christian attitudes in life. "Do not give dogs what is holy," is a saying

Matthew inserted into this section. Jesus was probably quoting a familiar saying of the time. "Don't burn yourself out on those who do not respond to the Gospel," is the gist of the saying.

We conclude our reading of the sermon on Saturday. *Do* the word, is Jesus' final admonition, don't just listen to it. If we're looking for comforting words that help us settle back into a self-satisfied lifestyle, the Sermon on the Mount will not be our cup of tea. This collection of Jesus' sayings was shared with converts to the Christian faith. This was their teaching about what it meant to be a follower of the risen Christ. It calls for a complete reorientation of life.

We leave Matthew as we come to the end of the Sermon on the Mount and turn next week to the Gospel of John, the traditional reading in the daily office lectionary during the Lenten season.

The week of Last Epiphany

The Old Testament readings:

Our reading in Deuteronomy last week included a rehearsal of the Ten Commandments. As our readings open this week, Israel is ordered to remember those commandments and the covenant with God. To remember and to follow the commandments is to prosper in the new land. Then comes the great statement of faith called the Shema, the Hebrew word meaning hear: "Hear, O Israel: The Lord our God is one Lord; and you shall love the Lord your God with all your heart, and with all your soul, and with all your might." (Deut. 6:4) These are the words that sum up the whole meaning of the covenant. They stand like a great creedal statement expressing the faithful Jew's faith in the one God.

The Shema was, and still is, on the lips of every faithful Jew from earliest childhood. These words are to be repeated to the next generation and written on one's clothing and on the doorposts of one's home. Israel is never to forget that God still provides for them as God provided for them in the wilderness. The problem for future generations is that when life gets easier for them, they may forget their total dependence on God.

The reference to Massah in Tuesday's reading recalls the lack of faith displayed by the Hebrews during a time of thirst. See Exodus 17:2-7 for the story.

We step out of Deuteronomy on Ash Wednesday in order to pick up the theme and feel of that important day. The city of Nineveh repented when they heard the preaching of Jonah. The king ordered a fast and special acts of penance.

God's choice of a people is by grace, we learn on Thursday. The Hebrews were not a strong and mighty nation. God chose them because God loved their ancestors, not because the Hebrew people were a great and worthy nation. (We see the same pattern in the choice of Jesus' disciples. He did not choose the rich and powerful, but the outcasts and working people of his day.) The blessings of the covenant are outlined for Israel, blessing that come with the keeping of the covenant. But those blessings are balanced with grim warnings for failure to live up to the covenant.

The Epistle readings:
We spend the first half of this week in the Epistle to the Hebrews. The writing is more of an exhortation or sermon than a letter. Written late in the first century, it was addressed to a church suffering from terrible persecution, a church that could easily lose faith if another wave of persecution were to hit. Though the unknown writer of the epistle was apparently addressing gentile Christians living in Rome, he used the language of the Temple sacrificial system to make some of his major points.

Keep in mind the gospel reading for last Sunday as you begin your reading in Hebrews this week. On the Mount of Transfiguration, the disciples see in a momentary vision the fullness of Christ.

The Letter to the Hebrews opens with these magnificent words: "In many and various ways God spoke of old to our fathers by the prophets; but in these last days he has spoken to us by a Son, whom he appointed the heir of all things, through whom also he created the world." (Heb. 1:1-2). Jesus is the fullness of the revelation of God, a suitable note to crown this epiphany theme with. Extensive quotations from the psalms are used by the writer of Hebrews to build his case that Jesus is a higher order of being even than the angels and certainly than any prophets who went before him. "He reflects the glory of God and bears the very stamp of his nature..." (Heb. 1:3). Jesus became fully man, one who lived a life "lower than the angels," and yet he was far greater than the angels. But, if he was to deliver people from their bondage and lead them to glory, then he must fully identify with their human condition. He must share in their sufferings if he is to redeem their sufferings and turn evil to good.

The reading from Hebrews appointed for Ash Wednesday picks up the theme of discipline so appropriate for the coming

Lenten season. As a parent demands discipline from a child, so God calls for discipline from us. "Therefore, since we are surrounded by so great a cloud of witnesses, let us also lay aside every weight, and sin which clings so closely, and let us run with perseverance the race that is set before us. . ." (Heb. 12:1). In the previous chapter the writer listed some of those great witnesses of faith whose stories are found in the Hebrew Scriptures. They are to be our models for faithful discipleship.

Titus is the third of the pastorals dealing with the concerns of a church gearing up for an on-going life in the present age.

Titus was a faithful disciple of Paul's. We catch glimpses of his relationship with Paul in Galatians 2:1, 3 and 2 Corinthians 8:6, 16-23. Though the letter opens with personal greetings to Titus from Paul, realize that the letter is really addressed to the whole emerging church providing guidelines for structure, discipline and Christian witness. Monday's reading includes criteria for choosing leaders that parallel the criteria found in the third chapter of 1 Timothy. See my comments in regard to that passage on Wednesday of the week of 6 Epiphany.

The second and third chapters of Titus read on Friday are a list of suggestions for leading the Christian life. Obedience to authority was. a concern for a young church trying to get along with the powers of the world.

The Gospel readings:

This week we begin the reading of the Gospel of John that will take us through the first half of the week of 2 Easter. The church has a long tradition of reading the Fourth Gospel at this time in the liturgical year.

Though the writer of the Gospel of John followed the pattern of the synoptic gospels, (Matthew, Mark and Luke) in recording the events of Jesus' life, death and resurrection, he departed radically from the gospel format in that his main interest was in giving the reader a theological interpretation of those events rather than in simply proclaiming them. John assumed that his readers knew what Jesus had said and done.

John used poetry, metaphor and symbolic language to write his theological statement of the Christ. When dealing with ultimate mystery, one must turn to poetry and symbolism to express the fullness of life that we can only begin to touch. As you read the long and intricate speeches of John in this gospel, realize that you are reading beautiful poetry that leads the Christian to an understanding of what stands behind the words and actions of Jesus.

The opening words of the Gospel of John serve as a beautiful overture to his whole work. The word, or wisdom, of God reaches out of eternity, becomes incarnate, so that people can know God intimately and personally in Jesus. Later in the gospel the powerful news is carried further. Through the Holy Spirit, God comes to each generation in the flesh of human encounter to touch men and women personally. God still dwells with us!

John the Baptist points beyond himself to Jesus, and at least two of John's disciples turn from John to Jesus. One of those disciples is the brother of Simon Peter. The Gospel of John often differs in the account of events from the synoptic gospels. Matthew, Mark and Luke report that Jesus calls Peter as he sees Peter at his fishing boat. In the Gospel of John, however, it is Peter's brother who brings Peter to see Jesus. John may have inherited different traditions about Jesus or he may have altered stories to express his theological understanding.

The term "lamb of God" appears in Thursday's lection. The title comes out of the Temple ritual.

Exodus 12 directs that an unblemished lamb be slaughtered at the Passover and consumed by the people. Lambs were also offered in sacrifice at other festival days at the Temple. The offering of the innocent lamb at Passover was seen as a way of becoming at-one with God again after the separation that the people had caused by their sinfulness. The sacrifice of the Paschal or Passover Lamb restored the people to God. The Passover was a pilgrim festival; persons came from all over the nation to share this feast in Jerusalem. They would enter the city and then go to the Temple, where they would buy a lamb from the sellers at the Temple grounds. The lamb was then offered in sacrifice. After the blood was sprinkled on the altar, the people would take the meat to their rented rooms, where it would be cooked and eaten as a part of the Passover meal.

. . . (Jesus) then offered himself as "a perfect sacrifice for the whole world." (Prayer of Consecration, Book of Common Prayer, page 362). The disciples came to realize that Jesus was the true Paschal Lamb that takes away the sins of the people by the forgiving love of God that he showed forth from the Cross and at the resurrection. (Joseph P. Russell, *Sharing our Biblical Story,* Minneapolis, Minn., Winston Press, 1979, pp. 151-152.)

Wednesday of this week of last Epiphany we read lessons appropriate for Ash Wedneday. Our prayers and penance must be sincere. We must offer our prayers not out of pride but out of humility.

Lent and the Daily Office Lectionary

In the primitive church, Lent was a time of final preparation for those who were to be baptized at Easter. Three years was the normative time for a person to spend in preparation for initiation into the church. During that time, candidates had heard the salvation story of the Hebrew Scriptures, the Good News as proclaimed in the Gospel accounts of Jesus, and the theological reflections of that Good News as outlined in the epistles of St. Paul and other early Christian leaders.

As their baptisms grew closer, the candidates began to see themselves as citizens of God's coming reign rather than as citizens of the Roman Empire. God's word and God's work formed a radical consciousness and demanded a radical obedience. Lent was the final preparation time. Like Jesus, they spent 40 days struggling with the temptations of evil and their own fears. Like their biblical ancestors of an earlier day they struggled in the wilderness, having been set free from the bondage of sin to move across the wilderness toward the promise of Christ's coming reign. The story of the exodus from Egypt became the personal story of every Christian convert. They took on added practices of obedience to the calling of Christ and they rehearsed, once again, the whole sweep of the salvation history.

Gradually, all the Christian community began to adopt the special call for obedience and to remembering the salvation story so that Easter became a time of renewed commitment to the covenant of baptism.

In this season of Lent, we are called back to the roots of our faith in Christ. We rehearse and remember the faith story, we practice the obedient life of a Christian disciple and we seek a fuller entrance into the life of Christ's Body, the church.

The readings from Hebrews that we are studying in our epistle readings during the first week of Lent match perfectly the readings from Deuteronomy also appointed for the first week. The Hebrew people, we are reminded in both sets of readings, were tested in the wilderness by God because of their unfaith-fulness. Lent is our annual time of testing, our wilderness wandering time in which we look again at the covenant made with our biblical ancestors and with each new generation.

The first week of Lent
Year One

The Old Testament readings:

God provided for our forebears during that long generation of wandering. God provides for us in our lives. As our people took the bread each day in the wilderness, they knew it was provided by God. There is no way they could have provided it for themselves. "And he humbled you and let you hunger and fed you with manna, which you did not know, nor did your fathers know; that he might make you know that man does not live by bread alone, but that man lives by everything that proceeds out of the mouth of the Lord." These were the words quoted by Jesus to Satan in the wilderness temptation. (Matt. 4:4). The wilderness experience was a humbling experience as the people found themselves totally dependent on God.

Tuesday's reading provides a warning that when we become self-sufficient we are not to forget who we are in relationship to God. The text is assigned to be read at the Eucharist on Thanksgiving Day, an appropriate time for our nation to be humbled in the face of prosperity so that we can remember who is most deserving of our thanksgiving.

The writer of Deuteronomy, speaking through the memory of Moses' last days with the Hebrews in the wilderness, goes on to remind the people that any success they may have as a nation is not their own doing but God's. Though the author of Deuteronomy does not use the word grace, that is certainly the concept he is expressing.

The reference in Thursday's reading to Israel's defiance at Kadesh-barnea recalls the fear of the people to move into the land of Canaan after spies sent to explore the land came back with the report that the inhabitants were strong and would be hard to defeat in battle. Despite Moses' promise that God was with them, they lacked the faith to take the land. Notice Moses' argument that he had used before God to spare the people. "You don't want to look silly before the other nations by having your people perish in the wilderness, do you?"

"And now, Israel, what does the Lord our God require of you, but to fear the Lord your God, to walk in all his ways, to love him, to serve the Lord your God with all your heart and with all your soul, and to keep the commandments and statutes of the Lord, which I command you this day for your good?" (Deut. 10:12-13) These words summarize the results of Israel's history with God. The response, moreover, is the response of justice to neighbor and stranger alike. Our baptismal covenant calls us to ". . . seek and serve Christ in all persons, loving your neighbor as yourself. . . (to) strive for justice and peace among all people, and respect the dignity of every human being."

The people can choose life or death by the way they respond to the covenant: "You shall therefore lay up these words of mine in your heart and in your soul; and you shall bind them as a sign upon your hand, and they shall be as frontlets between your eyes." (Deut. 11:18) These poetic words of commitment were literalized by later Jews. The phylacteries, mentioned by Jesus, were pouches worn by Jews at prayer. Part of today's reading, along with three other passages from the Torah, were carried in the pouches as a way of fulfilling this commandment. Many Jewish people to this day place a *mezuzah* on their front doorpost, a small metal plate containing the words of the Shema, "Hear, O Israel: The Lord our God is one Lord," (Deut. 6:4), fulfilling the command of Deuteronomy 11:20 that the words of God delivered to Moses must be placed on the doorposts of the homes. "And you shall teach them to your children, talking of them when you are sitting in your house, and when you are walking by the way, and when you lie down, and when you rise." (Deut. 11:19) This beautiful statement lies at the heart of our tradition of the daily office. We begin, live, and end with each day framed in God's word and covenant. It also calls us to teach the word of God to each new generation.

The Epistle readings:

At this time we read only chapters 1 through 5 and a section of chapter 12 of Hebrews. We'll read other selections the last part of the Easter season. In our present section the author is comparing Jesus to the high priest who served in the Temple of Jerusalem. The high priest could represent the people before God because he shared all of their struggles with sin. He was not aloof from the people's hurts and needs. Jesus, too, was fully human. He shares all our human sufferings as well as our joys: "For because he himself has suffered and been tempted, he is able to help those who are tempted." (Hebrews 2:18) The author inserts frequent quotations from the psalms and the prophets familiar to the first and second century readers.

Moses was considered the father of the house by the Jews for he had led the Hebrews out of Egypt toward the Promised Land. And yet Jesus is far greater in that household than Moses ever could be: "Yet Jesus has been counted worthy of as much more glory than Moses as the builder of a house has more honor than the house." (Hebrews 3:3) Christ is the heir of God. Moses is only the servant.

Tuesday's reading ends with a quotation from Psalm 95 that reminded the Jewish people that their ancestor's unfaithfulness had resulted in their wandering in the wilderness for a generation. The wilderness testing needs to be seen as a grim reminder to the Christian church in its time of severe testing in persecution, the writer says.

With Thursday's reading (Hebrews 4:1-10) the author shifts from the image of wilderness wandering to the metaphor of the Sabbath rest. He picks up this metaphor from the closing words of Psalm 95 that he quoted in Hebrews 3:7-11. The rest is the promised rest of the Sabbath decreed by God at creation (Gen. 2:2). The people's Sabbath rest will ultimately come as they enter with complete faith into God's promise.

The warning for unfaithfulness greets us again with the opening words in Friday's reading. Those words lead to a magnificent summary of the author's points made thus far in the epistle: "Since then we have a great high priest who has passed through the heavens, Jesus, the Son of God, let us hold fast our confession. For we have not a high priest who is unable to sympathize with our weaknesses, but one who in every respect has been tempted as we are, yet without sinning. Let us then with confidence draw near to the throne of grace, that we may receive mercy and find grace to help in time of need." (Hebrews 4:14-16)

On Saturday, we return to the metaphor of Christ as great high priest. He is a priest "after the order of Melchizedek." (Hebrews 5:6). This brief statement refers to a passage in Genesis 14:18-19: "And Melchizedek king of Salem brought out bread and wine; he was priest of God Most High. And he blessed (Abram). . ." Since this priest and king of Salem blessed Israel's great ancestor, obviously Melchizedek represented a higher order than the priests of the temple who traced their lineage through the levitical house of Aaron, the brother of Moses. Christ, being of that higher order of Melchizedek, takes precedence over the Temple priests. And because of his complete identification with the suffering of all people, he is the perfect high priest.

The Gospel readings:

The wedding of Cana in Galilee is our beginning point for this week's reading. This is a symbolic narrative. To know and accept the Christ is to be purified and begin a new life. The water of the old covenant becomes the finest wine of the new covenant. That point is repeated in Tuesday's reading when we read of Jesus going to cleanse the Temple in Jerusalem. The Temple must be purified, signifying the new life made known in Christ. The risen body of Christ, which is the church, will become the new meeting place between men, women and God, rather than the Temple in Jerusalem.

On Wednesday we read of a rather strange conversation between Jesus and Nicodemus, held by night to denote both the need for secrecy and a symbol of coming out of darkness into light. We see here a pattern in John's writing: Jesus talks with someone at a metaphorical level. The person hears Jesus' words at the literal level and, thus, fails to understand. The gospel writer then has Jesus explain the metaphor in an extended theological discourse.

Notice on Saturday this same pattern is followed as Jesus encounters the woman at the well. The living water Jesus refers to is a relationship with God revealed through Jesus Christ!

The second week of Lent

The Old Testament readings:

For the next four weeks of Lent we follow the long standing tradition of reading from the prophet Jeremiah. Jeremiah began his prophetic ministry in about the year 627 B.C. Josiah was king of Judah at the time. He had a deep commitment to the covenant and wanted to purify Judah's cultic and social life. The Book of Deuteronomy and the historic books of Joshua through Second Kings were written as a part of Josiah's reform movement. The books reflect the theology of the time. If Judah faithfully followed the values and commandments set forth in the Mosaic covenant, Judah would prosper. If the nation broke the covenant it would suffer adversity.

Part of the Deuteronomic understanding of that covenant was that Judah's worship must be centered in the Jerusalem Temple. Moreover, justice must be done for widow, orphan and the oppressed. Battles were won when the people obeyed God. Suffering resulted when the people forgot their covenant with God.

Legalism crept into the system along with a feeling that God would never let the Temple or nation fall. So long as Judah followed the Temple ritual, the reasoning went, God would protect the nation.

Jeremiah at first supported the reform movement of Josiah, but gradually became disillusioned as legalism replaced the freshness of reform. Josiah was killed in battle in 609 B.C., and his reforms died with him. Weaker kings followed Josiah, kings who had to face the growing menace of the mighty Babylonian armies sweeping across the eastern Mediterranean world. In 598 Jehoiakim became king only to have the Babylonians invade the land and deport the leaders of the land to exile in Babylonia. Jehoiakim's uncle, Zedekiah, replaced him and served as a vassal king to the Babylonians.

During these tragic times kings and court prophets had told the people that God would protect them. The Temple and God's city of Jerusalem would never fall to the hated enemy. Jeremiah's message stood in sharp contrast to the official word. He went through the streets announcing that it was God's will that the nation fall! After all, they had broken covenant time and again. Justice for the oppressed, compassion for the widow and orphan had long since been forgotten. Judah had worshipped other gods and forgotten the one god who had called Israel out of Egypt into the Promised Land. Rather than hold out against the Babylonians, the king should surrender. Jeremiah was not a popular man.

The Book of Jeremiah is an anthology of the prophet's work written and spoken over a time spanning the 13th year of King Josiah's reign in 627 B.C. when reform and confidence were high, to the year 587 when Zedekiah watched while his sons were killed before his eyes and then was blinded and led away captive to Babylonia. He had ignored the warnings and word of Jeremiah. He had ignored the covenant call to justice demanded by the Torah. Babylonia laid seige on Jerusalem and sent another wave of people into exile 11 years after the first people had left.

As noted above, Jeremiah has traditionally been read during Lent. The reason is obvious. The prophet's word calls us to look at our own society and see it through the eyes of God's covenant with us. We read history, true, but far more importantly we read words that call us to account as a people. Jeremiah's concerns must be our concerns. Our Lenten awareness of sin that calls us to repentance and reform is heightened as we walk the streets of Jerusalem with Jeremiah.

The Book of Jeremiah opens, appropriately enough, with Jeremiah's description of his call by God to be a prophet. (Compare it with Isaiah's call found in the sixth chapter of Isaiah.) God will put words in Jeremiah's mouth, words of authority and power. The early blooming plant described in Monday's reading is a sign that God is an early bloomer in the sense of looking ahead and understanding what is to come. A nation will threaten Judah from the north, and that threat is no historic accident; it is the will of God. Judah must be punished.

Tuesday's reading remembers with fondness the days of Israel's wilderness wandering. Then the people remembered God for they knew they had to rely each day on God's providence. Last week during our study of the Book of Deuteronomy we read a warning to the people. The people had gone after other Gods and forgotten their call to act justly in accordance with the covenant, Jeremiah reminded them.

Judah acted like a whore chasing after men on the hilltops and being unfaithful to her own spouse. Surely Judah should have taken warning from the fall of Israel to the Assyrian armies in 721 B.C. That should have chastened the wayward Judah, but no, the nation had continued to chase after other gods whose altars were usually placed on high hills. Jeremiah speaks for God as he pleads with the people to return. He does have one word of hope for the wayward Judah. After their punishment at the hand of Babylonia, God will restore them.

Watch for the vivid metaphors of impending doom outlined in Thursday's reading. Creation will be reversed, is the thrust of Jeremiah's lament: "I looked on the earth, and lo, it was waste and void; and to the heavens, and they had no light." (Jer. 4:23)

This second week of Lent we as the church of Christ need to look across our society as Jeremiah did.

The Epistle readings:

Paul's Epistle to the Romans will be our focus of study for the balance of Lent in the daily lectionary readings. Romans is Paul's most complete statement of the gospel. Romans was his primer in the Christian faith, written to people whom he longed to visit but had never met. He wrote an extended letter of introduction, making a place for himself in their midst when he could finally visit them. He would finally meet those people as a prisoner of the Roman government! It would appear that this letter was written while Paul was in Corinth planning a trip to deliver the money he had been collecting for the poor in Jerusalem. Thus the letter came late in his ministry and reflects his growing understanding of the gospel.

After Paul's greeting to the Romans, he moves quickly into stating his major thesis: "For I am not ashamed of the gospel; it is the power of God for salvation to every one who has faith, to the Jew first and also to the Greek. For in it the righteousness of God is revealed through faith for faith; as it is written, 'He who through faith is righteous shall live.'" (Romans 1:16-17)

Having stated his thesis, Paul next explains the need for the saving power of God. Everyone, Jew and gentile alike, has turned to wickedness, and all stand in judgment before God. Though the gentiles do not live under the law of the covenant, they have a natural law. They should be able to see God in the natural order of life and respond to the love and creativeness with faith and right actions.

Instead the people turn to self-worship and immoral practices. But the Jews, who felt that they should be considered righteous because they were circumcised and followed the other ritual acts of the covenant, are condemned even more severely than the gentiles, for the Law makes even clearer how far they have turned from God in sin. The Law, in other words, condemns rather than saves.

But, Paul points out, Christians must always remember that it was the Jews who were entrusted with the wisdom, or oracles, of God in the first place. It was the Jews who revealed God's word and presence, even in their unfaithfulness. God will be faithful to the covenant made with the Jews even if the people themselves have been unfaithful.

A familiar question raised in response to Paul's preaching occurs to him as he continues to write his letter: "If a person's sin helps to point up God's justice, should that person be condemned?" A second question grows out of the first: "If my wickedness and lying serve to make God look better, why should God be angry with me?" These were questions raised by Paul's audiences. He realizes that the people of Rome might have the same problems with his teachings. We will hear Paul's response to these concerns later on in chapters 6 and 8.

Friday's reading brings a somber note. All stand condemned, Jew as well as gentile. The Law that the Jew relies on for salvation only condemns the Jew by pointing up the sinfulness of each person.

On Saturday, we turn to the theme of justification by faith. Faith, for Paul, was an action word. I can jog, I can diet, but the true test of whether I'm really open to be healed (salved, saved) by a physician is whether I can put my life on the operating table. Faith results in action, in a changed life, in a total trust of God's power. Nothing can make us righteous before God but our faith.

Paul teaches that none of us can possibly earn God's grace. The Parable of the Prodigal Son (Luke 15:11-32) comes to mind. The younger son was accepted by the father even before the words begging for acceptance were out of his mouth. The reinstatement was offered freely. There could be no sense of pride for the younger son. He received his place only by the grace of his loving father.

If one sinned in biblical times, one had to pay for that sin with a sacrifice to God. An animal, a bird, or a grain offering had to be made. The offering paid for the sin of the offerer. The pure lamb offered at the Passover in the Temple died for the sins of the family offering the lamb. Its blood was a sign of covenant and forgiveness. Christ was the final sacrifice, made for the sins of everyone ever to be born, Paul stated. The idea of a God who would not demand some kind of payment was alien to Paul's way of thinking. A just God would have to receive payment.

The Gospel readings:

The cure of the nobleman's son, read on Tuesday, is the second of John's seven signs described in the gospel. Each sign becomes a further indication of Jesus' nature. To know Jesus is to experience eternal life, we read in John 17:3, and that life was happening as people grew to know Jesus in the signs of his love and power.

The third sign, or miracle, of Jesus is the cure of the sick man at the Pool of Bethesda, read on Wednesday. Notice again the pattern of dialogue that grows out of the healing act of Jesus. For a clearer understanding of the Gospel of John, read the discourses of Jesus as poetic statements of theology, rather than as actual speeches of Jesus.

Thursday's and Friday's readings interpret the Bethesda healing. We read John's theological understanding of the relationship between Jesus and God the Father. God's life-giving power is revealed through the Son. To listen to the Son is to hear the Father. Thus, to accept Jesus as the Son of God is to receive the eternal life offered by God the Father. Jesus is the source of life because God the Father is the ultimate source of life. (John 5:26) To reject Jesus is to reject God.

We skip over chapter 6 this week since that chapter is read two weeks from now to fit the theme of the Sunday collect. This moves us to chapter 7 where we again deal with the direct relationship between Jesus and God the Father. The chapter also shows the increasing hostility towards Jesus. Though some believe, many refuse to believe despite all the signs of Jesus' power and love. Even his own brothers do not have faith in him.

The third week of Lent

The Old Testament readings:

More words of God's anger directed toward Judah greet us as this third week of Lent begins. In this Lenten season we must ask ourselves how many of these words apply to our own society.

Part of Jeremiah's anguish was over the leaders of the nation who assured people that everything was just fine when in fact the very fabric of society was breaking apart and the marching steps of invading troops were coming closer: "For from the least to the greatest of them, everyone is greedy for unjust gain; and from prophet to priest, everyone deals falsely. They have healed the wound of my people lightly, saying, 'Peace, peace,' when there is no peace." (Jer. 6:13-15)

In the first year of Jehoiakim's reign in 609 B.C., Jeremiah warned the people that they could not rely on God to protect them just because they worshipped in the Temple. They must reform and return to the principles of the Torah.

Incidentally, Ephraim mentioned in verse 15 is another name for Israel, the northern kingdom, that was sent into exile by the Assyrians in 721 B.C.

In Wednesday's reading, Jeremiah writes as if the people are already in exile. The worst has happened and no matter where they turn they cannot find healing. Even in Gilead, a famous place of healing, there is no balm that will cure them.

Jeremiah turns from expressing disgust to pleading with God for mercy as the invading armies draw closer. At a time like this, he asks, how can people rely on carved images when Judah has been called forth by the God who creates the world and everything in it.

Some scholars feel that Friday's reading may have been written early in Jeremiah's career when he still supported Josiah's reforms. "Be faithful to the covenant," he wrote. The reading concludes with the anguished words of the prophet when he discovered that his own kinsmen in Anathoth were threatening to kill him. He felt like a sheep being led to slaughter, a vivid metaphor also found in Isaiah 53:7-8 where one who is a servant of God is described poetically. Philip interpreted Isaiah's words as applying to Jesus when he discussed the Isaiah passage with the Ethiopian eunuch in Acts 8:32.

The prophets often used symbolic actions as a means of conveying their message. In Saturday's reading Jeremiah hides a linen girdle for a long period of time. The decayed condition of the garment when he finds it sometime later becomes a sign of the impending decay of the nation as God acts in judgment against the people.

The Epistle readings:

I'd suggest taking a few minutes before reading Monday's and Tuesday's texts to look back at the stories of Abraham and Sarah in Genesis 12:1-9, 15:1-21, 17:1-27, and 18:1-15. The faith shown by Abraham became a model of the faith we are to have, and Abraham showed that faith generations before there was the Law of the covenant!

God's unbelievable grace that leads to human liberation and freedom from enslavement to sin becomes the focal point for the balance of the week. In the healing love of Jesus Christ came the realization that God's love is far more powerful than human sin or any evil that comes into the world. Adam is the symbol for the sinful nature of every man and woman. Christ is the living experience of God's forgiving grace.

Well, if our sinfulness serves to point up God's goodness, shall we not sin all the more? "Of course not," responds an indignant Paul. When we are baptized, we entered into Christ's death. We died to our old sinful ways. And when we were baptized, we entered into the new resurrected life of the risen Christ. How can we talk of going back to what we are dead to, Paul wonders.

The words spoken by priest or bishop at the time of baptism reflect Paul's theology of baptism: "We thank you, Father, for the Water of Baptism. In it we are buried with Christ in his death. By it we share in his resurrection. Through it we are reborn by the Holy Spirit. (BCP, p. 306).

"For the wages of sin is death, but the free gift of God is eternal life in Christ Jesus our Lord." (Romans 6:23). These beautiful words of Paul's conclude our week in Romans.

The Gospel readings:

Growing conflict over Jesus is the theme of the readings for Monday and Tuesday of this week. Notice that most of the actions of Jesus and the discourses of John explaining the significance of those actions come in connection with the major Jewish festivals. Some scholars feel that the writer of the Gospel of John used the Jewish festivals as a framework so that gospel would be seen as a Christian commentary on the true meaning of the traditional Jewish festivals. Jesus came to cleanse the old Law, the Temple, the festivals and the people of faith. This basic message of John's Gospel is said in as many different ways as the writer can conceive.

In any case, the action of chapter 7 centers on the feast of Tabernacles. Jesus confronts the ultimate authority of the Torah, that guided every action and thought of the faithful Jew, with the new Word or Torah from God, Jesus himself. He is the new living Law of God. The "living water" theme from chapter 3 read the first week of Lent is picked up again in Tuesday's reading: "If any one thirst, let him come to me and drink."

On Wednesday we move to another metaphor that helps to describe the role of Jesus in the world: "I am the light of the world; he who follows me will not walk in darkness, but will have the light of life." (John 8:12)

For the balance of the week we continue reading the dialogue between Jesus and the unbelieving Jews. His words are blunt and confrontational. Though there is no doubt that Jesus confronted the Jews with strong words in his lifetime, the words we read here are most likely statements of the early church directed toward the Jews of the second century and written to encourage the new gentile Christians who were coming into the church.

The Jews had rejected the Christ and, therefore, the promise was now passed on to those who could accept the signs of Jesus and become his followers. Christians were being persecuted by the time the Gospel of John was written. Though the first Christians were Jews, by the time this gospel was written the church was largely gentile. Hatred of Jews because of the persecutions was high. The writer of the Gospel of John reflects that hatred in his writings, and he is also concerned to explain to the gentiles why the Jews had not accepted Jesus as the Christ.

Unfortunately, these strong words of condemnation of the Jews have been used throughout these 2,000 years of history to spread hatred for the Jews. It is important to read the gospel in the context of the time that it was written. Jesus loved the Jews who were his own people. In the Epistle to the Romans that we are reading in this season, Paul reminded his readers that Christians were only offered salvation in order ultimately to bring salvation to the Jews.

To live in the truth that Jesus brings is to be a free person, in contrast to living under the enslavement of sin. The Jews would argue that their relationship of freedom with God was guaranteed because they were children of the Mosaic covenant. Jesus' words echo John the Baptist's statement in Matthew 3:9: "God is able from these stones to raise up children of Abraham," John had said. Here the writer of the Gospel of John points out that a person's relationship to God is really judged by one's actions. In this case the necessary action is love for Jesus and faith that he, indeed, is the Son of God. Incidentally, Jesus' frequent use of the words, "I AM" to identify himself was to play on the mysterious name of God revealed to Moses in Exodus 3:14, "I AM WHO I AM. . .I AM has sent me to you." When Jesus said he was I AM he meant that he himself was God. No wonder the Jews picked up stones to throw at him! (John 8:59)

The fourth week of Lent

The Old Testament readings:

In Sunday's reading, Jeremiah takes the natural event of a drought and sees it as a sign of God's wrath, No one need ask why there is so much suffering, Jeremiah tells the people. The answer is obvious from Judah's behavior.

The time will soon come, we read in Monday's lesson, when the people will no longer look back to the exodus from Egypt as the crucial saving event of God. In the future, people will look back to the time when God restores the people and brings them back from exile in Babylonia.

Jeremiah sees another sign of God's future activity as he observes a potter working at his wheel. God deals with Judah in the way that a potter handles clay on the wheel. As the potter can reshape the clay that is being formed on the wheel, so can God make new the nation of Israel. A vivid description of the unjust economic practices of Judah is the focus of Thursday's reading, a reminder to us that the church must be concerned for economic justice.

After chastising the present shepherds of Judah (the kings and leaders of the land) for not being good shepherds, God promises to send a true shepherd in the future. Jeremiah is referring to a future king, "a righteous branch" of King David. Words such as these were applied to Jesus by the early church. In John 10, Jesus is called the Good Shepherd who comes to lay down his life for the people. Jesus' life, death and resurrection were seen within the context of the Hebrew Scriptures.

After castigating the kings, Jeremiah turns in Saturday's reading to condemn the prophets who led the people astray with false promises of security. All these prophets shall be cut down.

The Epistle readings:

The Law of Torah does not make one righteous, Paul points out. The Law is defeating and not life-giving. All the Law does is to convict one of sin by making the sin clearer.

When I see the 35-mile-per-hour speed limit sign, it convicts me of my sin as I glance at my speedometer and find I'm doing 55. The blue flashing lights in the rear view mirror announce that judgment is near, but the sign has not saved me from the sin. Moreover, the Law awakens the sinful desire within me.

As Paul reflected on the Law of the Torah and the attempts to make himself righteous, he finally threw up his hands in despair. The harder he tried to do what was right, the more he stood hopelessly convicted of his sinfulness. It's as if there were an unseen power within him placing him in alienation with his own being as well as with God. What was he to do?

Freed from sin, we're filled with the Holy Spirit. We are not left at the mercy of sinful impulse. We are not free to sin so that grace may abound. We have a new destiny in the Spirit, and the Spirit dwelling within us makes us sons and daughters of God. We can actually address the awesome God as Abba, or Daddy. Now nothing can separate us from the love of God.

Paul draws on his personal experience of suffering from pain and persecution to make generalizations about the redeeming quality of suffering that all Christians share. Moreover, the struggles of the present will give way to the birth of the new age. Our present pain is like the pangs of a woman in childbirth. All creation cries out, anxiously awaiting the birth that is coming!

Incidentally, Romans 8:14-19, along with additional verses from chapter 8, are appointed in the Book of Common Prayer for reading at a burial.

Though Paul talks as if sin were defeated, he also points forward to the time when this reality will finally be fulfilled. There is a "here, but not yet" quality to what Paul writes in Romans. Sin is defeated, and we have a new master in the Holy Spirit. We can call God our Abba and be free from slavery to sin, and we are really living in expectant hope of final victory.

The Holy Spirit leads the Christian to cry out Abba. It is the Spirit who makes those words possible for us to say, since it is the Spirit who makes the Christian a daughter or son of God. In the same way, the Spirit groans within us so that we can communicate with God in ways that we cannot even comprehend. God knows the words of the Spirit, thus the Spirit is able to say for us what we do not have the power, courage, or insight to pray for ourselves.

A note of predestination is heard on Friday: "For those whom he foreknew he also predestined to be conformed to the image of his Son..." (Romans 8:29). The term, predestination, is often used erroneously to mean that God orders certain things to happen and certain people to be saved, while condemning others to damnation. Paul used this term simply to say that God called out the church from among the peoples of the world to witness to the risen Christ and to share in his death and resurrection. Before Christ, Israel had been the one destined to witness to God's presence and power in the world.

The Gospel readings:

The fourth Sunday of Lent has traditionally been known as Refreshment Sunday. In the early church the pope distributed bread to the poor on this Sunday in Lent so that the story of Jesus feeding the 5,000 soon became associated with the day. The strict Lenten discipline was lifted at this mid-Lent time. (*The Oxford American Prayer Book Commentary,* Massey Shepherd, Oxford University Press, 1950, pp. 130-131.) The collect appointed for this Sunday expresses the theme:

"Gracious Father, whose blessed Son Jesus Christ came down from heaven to be the true bread which gives life to the world; Evermore give us this bread, that he may live in us, and we in him; who lives and reigns with you and the Holy Spirit, one God, now and for ever." (BCP p. 219)

It is for this reason that we read the sixth chapter of the Gospel of John during this entire week. The gospel lessons provide a running commentary on the meaning of the story of the feeding of the 5,000. The first 15 verses of the chapter describe the event and the rest of the chapter is a poetic theological explanation of the meaning of the story.

Our readings this week have definite Eucharistic overtones: "...he who eats my flesh and drinks my blood has eternal life..." (John 6:54). Some scholars feel that John 6:51-58 was originally part of the Last Supper narrative in chapter 13 and later was moved to this position to enlarge on the theme of Jesus as the bread of life. The chapter provides a beautiful sacramental statement of the Eucharist. Read it with the Book of Common Prayer open beside your Bible, comparing the great thanksgiving of the Eucharist with the words of the Gospel of John. (See BCP pp. 362-363, 368-375.)

The fifth week of Lent

The Old Testament readings:

In Sunday's reading, we continue with Jeremiah's words of condemnation of the false prophets of Judah who speak words of encouragement to the people. Those words are not God's words, Jeremiah proclaims. They are words that raise false hopes at a time when the people need to be confronted with the cost of the sinfulness.

The strong Lenten theme of judgment is implicit in everything that Jeremiah says. His words must lead us to ask who the false prophets are today in church and in society?

On Monday we read of Jeremiah's vision of the two baskets of figs. The good figs are the people who were exiled to Babylonia in 598. Those who remain under King Zedekiah are the basket of poor figs. Judah must not put her hope on those who remain in the land, but rather on those who are in exile!

Chapter 25 read on Tuesday and Wednesday is a summary of the words spoken by Jeremiah up to the fourth year of Jehoiakim or 605 B.C. They may have been added by a later editor as a way of bringing a section of Jeremiah's writings to a close or they may have been composed as a conclusion to the scroll presented to Jehoiakim in December of 605. Read chapter 36 of Jeremiah for a description of how Jeremiah's words were received by the king at that time.

On Thursday, we shift from hearing Jeremiah's words to reading about his life. He suffered from the rejection of his own people because he felt that he had to speak God's word regardless of the cost. Years later Peter and the apostles would suffer persecution from the same conviction.

"Settle down, support your Babylonian captives. Marry, raise families, and make the best of things. You are going to be in this land for a long time. Don't get your hopes up about any rebellions back home in Judah that will end this exile." This was Jeremiah's message to the exiles. But notice the words of encouragement included with the admonitions to settle down:

"You will see me and find me; when you seek me with all your heart, I will be found by you, says the Lord, and I will restore your fortunes and gather you from all the nations, and all the places where I have driven you, says the Lord, and I will bring you back to the place from which I sent you into exile." (Jer. 29:13-14) Look at the contrast between these words of hope written by Jeremiah and the words of utter despair written by one who was living in Babylonian exile: "By the waters of Babylon, there we sat down and wept, when we remembered Zion. On the willows there we hung up our lyres. For there our captors required of us songs, and our tormentors, mirth, saying, 'Sing us one of the songs of Zion!' How shall we sing the Lord's song in a foreign land?" (Psalm 137:1-4)

Jeremiah made a shocking statement to such captives and to the people who remained behind in what was left of Judah. You *can* sing the Lord's song. You *can* pray to God, and you can know God wherever you are. God is not tied to a piece of land called Judah, nor to a Temple in Jerusalem. We experience a major leap in theological understanding with this passage from Jeremiah. Incidentally, life in Babylonia was obviously not all that bad. People could raise families and lead a good life in exile. As a matter of fact, many people chose not to return to Judah when they were freed under the Persian King Cyrus at the end of the exile.

Our Lent has been framed in the strong words of judgment from the Book of Jeremiah. Now on this Saturday of the fifth week of Lent we turn from judgment to hope. Jeremiah speaks of a new day when God will restore Judah. God will make a new covenant with the people, not written on stone but written instead on their hearts.

The Epistle readings:

Paul's deep love for the Jews causes him to turn his attention to their status under the gospel. Chapters 9 through 11 deal with this issue. First, Paul recalls seven privileges, or gifts, given to Israel. The list concludes with the gift of the Messiah, or

Christ. But what happened to this promise, if it has now been taken from Israel and given to the Christians? Drawing from a brief survey of the patriarchs of Israel, Paul reminds his readers that God can show mercy and love to whomever he chooses. Those who would question God must realize that the creature cannot possibly fathom the mind of the creator, any more than the pot can question the potter.

We can hear Paul's adversaries raising questions as we begin Monday's reading. "If God directs people in their actions, including 'hardening their hearts,' then how in the world can people be blamed for their sinful actions?" was the plaintive question Paul must have had directed to him time and again as he preached the Gospel. One cannot question God, Paul responds strongly. Be excited, rather, that God is showing mercy and grace in the midst of life's struggles. Paul speaks with sadness. The very "stone" that could bring the Jews salvation instead has become a stumbling block. Paul borrows the metaphor of the stone from Psalm 118 and applies it to Jesus.

Tuesday's selection contains the church's earliest creed. "Jesus is Lord," was the simple statement of the Christians. (Romans 10:9 and see also Phil. 2:11.) By the middle of the second century that three-word creed had expanded into the Apostles' Creed, a statement of faith made by candidates for baptism.

On the last three days of this fifth week of Lent we read the 11th chapter of Romans where Paul reveals the mystery of God's plan of salvation. The hearts of the Jews were hardened by God so that they would not preceive the Christ and know the love and mercy of God. But the salvation of the gentiles, in turn, would eventually cause the Jews to accept Christ. God's mercy would be revealed to them as well.

Paul uses quotations from the Hebrew Scriptures to fortify his point. Elijah despaired that there were any faithful people left in Israel at the time he fled Jezebel's wrath and went into the wilderness. God assured him that there was, indeed, a faithful remnant who would take up the witness of God. (1 Kings 19) The church, the Body of Christ, is the new remnant. But Christians had better be humble as they find themselves caught up in this divine plan. They were chosen by the grace of God and not by anything they had done. They are grafted onto the consecrated root that is Israel, a root that cannot lose its favored calling by God despite the unfaithfulness of the people over countless generations. God still loves the Jews and when they are finally restored it will be a glorious day.

The Gospel readings:

On Monday and Tuesday we read of the sixth sign of Jesus, the healing of the man born blind. This healing act becomes the opportunity for the writer of the gospel to reflect on the meaning of Jesus as the "light of the world." To know Jesus and to accept him as Son of God is truly to see.

Wednesday we read the beautiful metaphor of Jesus as the good shepherd. Well known words of faith are found in verse 10:10, "...I came that they may have life, and have it abundantly." The good shepherd discourse continues on Thursday. Opposition from the Jews leads to their attempt again to stone Jesus. Stoning was the penalty for blasphemy. Many of the words we read these weeks in John certainly sound like blasphemy! Jesus, after all, claimed to be one with the Father.

We turn to the seventh and final sign of Jesus on Friday and Saturday, as we read the story of the raising of Lazarus. This act leads to Jesus' powerful statement, "I am the resurrection and the life, he who believes in me, though he die, yet shall he live, and whoever lives and believes in me shall never die." (John 11:25-26). This final sign is a physical carrying out of Jesus' words in John 5:28: "...for the hour is coming when all who are in the tombs will hear his voice and come forth..." The event points to the full meaning of Jesus' life among the people and to the presence of the risen Christ among all people. Technically, this is not a resurrection account. Lazarus was brought back to life in this present age, but the story serves to dramatize the theological statements the writer of John has been making in the preceding chapters.

The lectionary provides an option on Friday and Saturday of reading the account of the anointing of Jesus by Mary at

Bethany and words summarizing the significance of the signs that Jesus has been performing among the people: "He who believes in me, believes not in me but in him who sent me. And he who sees me sees him who sent me. I have come as light into the world, that whoever believes in me may not remain in darkness."

Holy Week

We owe the ancient traditions of Holy Week to Bishop Cyril of Jerusalem who, in the fourth century, developed a way of helping the many pilgrims who visited Jerusalem at the Easter season experience the events of Jesus' passion and resurrection.

Bishop Cyril provided a way in which pilgrims could walk with Jesus in his last moments of life so that they "might walk in newness of life." So it was that each day leading up to Easter Sunday, the good bishop led pilgrims to places associated with events that led to Jesus' passion and resurrection. At each station, or place, the people participated in acts of remembrance and devotion, acts that became sacred drama helping the people live into the events they remembered.

Pilgrims gathered on the Sunday before Easter at the place where Jesus had entered Jerusalem. They waved palms and shouted glad Hosannahs as the bishop, mounted on a donkey, entered the city. Prayers were offered, and hymns of praise were sung as the people moved into the city with the bishop. And so it went each day. The whole drama culminated with the great vigil of Easter.

Keep this ancient tradition in mind as you walk through this week with the daily office and the other traditions of Holy Week carried out in your parish. The Eucharistic lectionary and the daily lectionary carry on the traditions begun by Cyril. Following Palm Sunday in the Eucharistic lectionary we move to the anointing of Jesus at Bethany on Monday, the cleansing of the Temple on Tuesday and the betrayal of Judas on Wednesday. Maundy Thursday, Good Friday and Holy Saturday lead us on our pilgrimage beyond cross and burial to the celebration of the resurrection on Easter Day.

Ritual and word must be lived out as we enter into the passion of Christ who suffers for the world. Think of men and women who enter into the struggles for justice and live the compassionate life. Look carefully at your own witness as a Christian and at the witness of your congregation. Prepare yourselves this sacred Holy Week to move out in your thinking and acting as well as into your thoughts and feelings.

Holy Week
Year One

The Old Testament readings:

During the third week of Lent we read of a plot by Jeremiah's own kinsmen to kill him. Our reading this Monday follows on the heels of that plot. Jeremiah cried out to God asking a question associated with the Book of Job. Why is it that the wicked prosper and the righteous suffer? Jeremiah is thinking of his own plight in the face of so much wickedness. God's answer is heard in Jeremiah 12:5: "If you have raced with men on foot, and they have wearied you, how will you compete with horses? And if in a safe land you fall down, how will you do in the jungle of the Jordan?" In other wrods, don't get discouraged, Jeremiah. You haven't seen anything yet! Even as God speaks into the mind of Jeremiah, "your brothers and the house of your father" are plotting against you.

Tuesday's passage is a dialogue between Jeremiah and God. The prophet cries out wishing that he had never been born. Speaking God's word has brought such pain. God promises to be with him and to strengthen him, if the prophet continues to speak the truth.

A collection of Jeremiah's sayings are read midweek. Jeremiah 17:8 reflects the wisdom of Psalm 1. The one who places confidence in God will be like the tree planted by the stream. What makes the writings of Jeremiah so powerful is the personal nature of much of what he says. On Maundy Thursday as we think of Jesus' total rejection for speaking and living the word of God, we hear Jeremiah's cry to God. Being God's prophet has meant utter rejection and ridicule. The word has brought Jeremiah to the brink of despair, and yet he can see a time when people will realize the power of God who has placed those words in his mouth.

The readings for Good Friday and Holy Saturday also reflect what is happening in the Eucharistic lectionary. As Jesus dies on the cross we are asked to remember that Abraham and Sarah's only son Isaac carried the wood for his own death by sacrifice up the hill of Moriah. The optional reading from the apocryphal Book of Wisdom expresses the hatred that persons caught up in evil have for the righteous. Job's words of complete trust in God's final vindication are familiar to many Episcopalians from their use as a part of the entrance rite in the Burial of the Dead: "For I know that my Redeemer lives, and at last he will stand upon the earth." (Job 19:25)

The Epistle readings:

Monday through Wednesday we read from the third and fourth chapters of Paul's Letter to the Philippians. If you want background on the historic context of this letter, read Acts 16:11-40. Paul may have written it from prison at Ephesus or Rome.

Despite his imprisonment, Paul writes with a sense of joy and gratitude for what the Philippians have done to support him and for their growing faith in God. His only concern is that he has heard there are some in the church who are trying to convince the people that they must adopt the strict ritualistic provisions of the Jews in order to be followers of Christ. Paul warns his friends to avoid such demands.

This concern to combat the Judaizers is evident in Monday's reading. Paul now counts everything he has "earned" as a Jew under the old Laws as worthless in his new relationship with the risen Christ. Now, nothing else matters: "All I care for is to know Christ, to experience the power of his resurrection, and to share his sufferings, in growing conformity with his death if only I may finally arrive at the resurrection from the dead." (Phil. 3:10-11, New English Bible.)

The catechumens who came as pilgrims in Bishop Cyril's time were there to share Christ's sufferings. Our Holy Week experience needs to be seen in the same light.

The epistle reading for Maundy Thursday speaks of the importance of the Eucharist. Paul gives a grim warning to those who participate in the Eucharist unworthily. In Paul's day, the Eucharist was part of a full meal. The church gathered for Eucharist as we would gather for a parish potluck.

Paul's anger stems from his observance that the Corinthians totally ignore one another's needs at these Eucharistic gatherings. Our Eucharistic rite reflects Paul's words. Before we receive the sacrament we examine ourselves in public confession. Following the absolution, we pass the peace of God's forgiveness to one another. If, for any reason, we find that we are not at peace with neighbor or stranger, then we are not fit to participate in the sacrament.

(There are times, especially during the season of Easter, when the confession is not said. The passing of the peace, however, is an integral part of the Eucharistic rite.)

Some scholars feel that the First Letter of Peter is actually composed of fragments of an early baptismal liturgy. The portion of First Peter assigned for Good Friday may be a prebaptismal homily delivered to the catechumens moments before their baptism. In any case, the meaning of our participation in Christ's death becomes clear. We have been ransomed by Christ. Therefore, "You shall be holy, for I am holy." (1 Peter 1:15). For comments about Saturday's readings, refer to my remarks made in connection with Thursday's and Friday's readings in the first week of Lent.

The Gospel readings:

We continue in our sequential reading of the Gospel of John on the first three days of Holy Week. The raising of Lazarus from the dead leads to Jesus' triumphal entry and a new determination on the part of the Jews to get rid of Jesus. Tuesday's reading is a beautiful statement of the meaning, not only of Jesus' death, but of our own as well: ". . .unless a grain of wheat falls into the earth and dies, it remains alone; but if it dies, it bears much fruit." (John 12:24). These scenes in Jerusalem offer the writer of the gospel an opportunity to express again the theological implications of Jesus' life, death, and resurrection. Jesus is the light that comes into the world. Can we dare to choose to live in darkness when the light has come? The last half of chapter 12 echoes the opening words of the Gospel of John, but the words take on a new significance as we move with Jesus into his final struggle.

Maundy Thursday's gospel reading is the great prayer for the church that the gospel writer attributes to Jesus as a part of his final words to the disciples at the Last Supper. We might say that it is a prayer of consecration for the church. Jesus consecrates the disciples in the way that a priest consecrates bread and cup at the Eucharist: "Sanctify them in the truth; thy word is truth. As thou didst send me into the world, so I have sent them into the world. And for their sake I consecrate myself, that they also may be consecrated in truth." (John 17:17-19)

The opening words in the next text, "Father, the hour has come; glorify thy Son that the Son may glorify thee. . ." (John 17:1), may sound strange in the context of Jesus' imminent death. "Glory" and "glorify" carry a technical meaning in the Gospel of John and in Hebrew literature: "The concept of the glory of God in OT thought offers important background for Johannine use. In the OT there are two important elements in the understanding of the glory of God; it is a *visible* manifestation of His majesty in *acts of power.* While God is invisible, from time to time He manifests Himself to men by striking action, and this is His *kabod* or glory." (*The Gospel According to John, The Anchor Bible,* volume 29, Raymond E. Brown, p. 503.) This is the glory Jesus prays for, that God's presence may become visible in an act of power realized through Jesus' death and resurrection.

The gospel readings for Good Friday help to set the theme and mood for this awesome day in the Christian calendar.

No gospel reading is assigned for Saturday.

The first week of Easter

The church's celebration of Easter begins with the first Eucharist of Easter Day and continues through the feast of Pentecost, 50 days later. During this time, we concentrate on the significance and joy of the resurrection. Just as one seventh of each week is focused on the resurrection with the celebration of Sunday, so a seventh of each year is focused on the meaning of the resurrection.

The Great 50 Days, as the Easter season has been traditionally called, was a means the primitive church used to bring the newly baptized into the life and witness of the church. Where Lent helped prepare the catechumens for their baptism, the Great 50 Days was a time of intensive teaching and training so that the newly baptized could understand how to lead the Christian life. This was, therefore, a time of great celebration as well as a time for instruction and sharing in the ministry and life of the church.

The Old Testament readings:
This week in the Old Testament we have a potpourri of selections that reflect the hope the Jews had for God's restoration of the nation. Even though the readings predate the resurrection, they can be appreciated in the light of the resurrection faith for they speak of God's power that turns the dark time of death into the new life.

We begin on Monday with a psalm of thanksgiving from the Book of Jonah. Though applied to Jonah at the moment he was saved from drowning by the great fish, this poem could have circulated independently as a psalm of praise to God who brings life out of death.

The theme of life out of death is picked up again on Tuesday as we read a psalm of hope from Isaiah, and on Wednesday as we move to the writings of the prophet Micah. Micah wrote of the promise of Judah's restoration despite the worst fears of her people and the gloating triumph of her enemies: ". . .when

I fall, I shall rise; when I sit in darkness, the Lord will be a light to me." (Micah 7:8)

The familiar vision of the dry bones, a powerful metaphor from Ezekiel, is assigned for Thursday. This passage is not a reference to the resurrection. Rather, the dry bones symbolize the despair of the nation after the return from exile in Babylonia. God's spirit will fill the people and their dry bones shall take on flesh and rise up in hope with a new vision of destiny.

On Friday we encounter what some scholars feel is the first mention of the hope of resurrection found in the Old Testament: "And many of those who sleep in the dust of the earth shall awake, some to everlasting life. . ." (Daniel 12:2a) The hope of the resurrection is a late development in Old Testament thought. Here we see the seed of a whole new understanding of God's power, realized in the resurrection of Jesus.

We round out our week of Old Testament readings with a vision of the messianic banquet. This reference to the banquet prepared for us in the kingdom is a fitting climax to our Easter week readings in the Old Testament, as well as a preparation for the Eucharist in the morning.

The second readings:

The second readings are taken from the Book of the Acts of the Apostles, in which we trace the impact of the resurrection and the coming of the Holy Spirit on the disciples. From completely demoralized men and women, the followers of Jesus become emboldened, Spirit-filled people who display the power of healing and speaking that Jesus promised them.

In Monday's reading we see an example of how the church quickly began using portions of Hebrew scripture as proof texts in teaching about the risen Christ. The writer of Acts took Psalm 16:8-11 as proof that King David foresaw the resurrection of Jesus the Christ and that, therefore, the Jews should have recognized Jesus' resurrection when it happened. If you read the entire psalm, you will see that it is a psalm of trust in the power of God to protect one. As the early church reflected on the meaning and power of the resurrection, Hebrew scripture was interpreted in an entirely new light.

The Gospel readings:

Our Gospel readings this week are words the writer of John attributed to Jesus as he prepared his disciples for his death and resurrection and their life as his Spirit-filled apostles.

Jesus goes to prepare a place for us, we hear on Monday. Jesus' death and resurrection point the way for us. Christians will do even greater works than Jesus is a second theme coming out of the assigned readings. The power shown by the apostles was the gift of the Holy Spirit promised by Jesus.

On Wednesday we read the beautiful poem of the vine. Jesus is the true vine, and we are but the branches. Cut off from the vine we can do nothing. This is both the hope and the warning given the postresurrection church. To be vine-like is to love as Jesus loved. That is the new commandment for the church. Easter Week is an appropriate time to hear once again the vision of the church that Jesus held out to his disciples. We must read these words today as the basis of our understanding of what life in the church of Christ means. From this vision of the church we move to warnings of persecutions. To be a follower of the risen Christ means that one will encounter rejection and suffering. By the time the Gospel of John was written the church was already experiencing the persecutions of a threatened culture. The warnings of Jesus would have been words of strength to those facing the temptation to recant the faith of Christ. May we be aware of Christians in the world today who suffer persecution, remembering that the vision of God's kingdom stands in such contrast to the present age that to proclaim the kingdom is to meet resistance from those who hold power. If the church is not facing resistance and conflict, then we must be careful, lest we have muted the call to live truly and proclaim the Gospel.

The second week of Easter

The Old Testament readings:

The Book of Daniel will be our companion for the next two weeks. Though the book refers to a time in history when our biblical ancestors were in exile in Babylonia (from about 586 to 538 B.C.), it was actually written during the time of Greek occupation of Judah, around 164 B.C. Daniel is not a historical book; it is a book composed partly of stories and partly of visions written for a people living under the domination of an alien culture. When the Greeks entered Judah during the fourth century before Christ, they promised leniency for those Jews who would give up their ancient practices and accept the culture and life view of the conquering armies. The Jews were tempted to adopt the Greek culture, both because they feared persecution if they kept to their Jewish practices and because the Greek way of life was attractive in the face of the rather austere Jewish customs of the time. Judaism faced a severe test.

In this painful time the Book of Daniel was written to encourage the people to keep the faith of their ancestors and to stand bravely in the face of persecution. The first six chapters of Daniel, assigned for reading, are heroic stories depicting the faith of four brave Jews who lived during the time of the Babylonian exile.

The story opens on Monday. Daniel and his three companions insist on keeping the dietary laws of Judaism, much to the concern of the chief eunuch responsible for them. The drama heightens when the king has a frightening dream and demands an explanation from the sages of the land. The fact that the king won't tell the wise men what his dream was adds to their plight. Not only must they interpret the dream, they must discover what the dream was! Though an impossible task for a mere Babylonian (also referred to as Chaldaeans), the challenge offers an opportunity to proclaim the power of the one God of Judah for Daniel. He both reveals and interprets the dream for the king and is given high office in the kingdom as a result.

Another adventure story is read on Wednesday and Thursday, the well-known story of Daniel's companions in the fiery oven. Shadrach, Meshach, and Abednego dance in the flames, ridiculing the impotence of the king in the face of God's power to save.

These are fitting stories of faith for us in this Easter season. We, too, face the temptations of an alien culture. How easy it is to compromise the Gospel and to receive the transitory rewards of the present age.

The Epistle readings:

Along with the Book of Daniel, we'll be reading the First Epistle of John the next two weeks. First John is a late New Testament writing, coming from the same hand, or at least the same school of writing, as the Gospel of John. The author of the epistle saw the church tempted to compromise the Gospel in the face of growing resistance and heretical teaching. The epistle calls the church back to the Gospel as it had originally been received, and it reminds the church in strong words that to follow Christ is to love and serve his people in the world.

The collect for the Second Sunday of Easter helps to set the tone for the Epistle readings this week: "...Grant that all who have been reborn into the fellowship of Christ's Body may show forth in their lives what they profess by their faith..." (BCP, p. 224)

Monday's reading has the feel of the first 18 verses of the Gospel of John. You may want to read those opening words to appreciate the place that 1 John has in the New Testament. On Tuesday you will read words that may be familiar to you, as they are a part of the comfortable words offered as an option after the confession in Rite I of the Holy Eucharist:

"...if any one does sin, we have an advocate with the Father, Jesus Christ the righteous; and he is the expiation for our sins, and not for ours only but also for the sins of the whole world." (1 John 2:1-2)

The ethical implications of this epistle as it reflects the meaning of the Gospel are made clear in Tuesday's reading: "He who says he is in the light and hates his brother is in the darkness still." (1 John 2:9) We cannot claim a personal relationship with the risen Christ and hate our neighbor and brother. (Jesus' words from the Sermon on the Mount expand this commandment: "But I say to you, love your enemies and pray for those who persecute you..." (Mt. 5:44a)

Those baptized into the Body of Christ at Easter were anointed with oil as a part of the baptismal ritual. Christians are not to forget their anointing and what it meant, we are reminded in Thursday's reading: "...as his anointing teaches you about everything, and is true, and is no lie, just as it has taught you, abide in him." (1 John 2:27b)

Our reading from 1 John ends the week with a strong reminder of the ethical imperative inherent in the Gospel. What has been handed on to us is the command to love as Christ loved—an active, vital, self-giving love. If we see someone in need and do not respond, then God's love cannot be in us for all the talk of being Spirit-filled.

In the lectionary and worship of the church, Easter must be seen as a baptismal renewal time for each Christian, as well as a time of including newly baptized Christians into the Body. We see in these readings a vision of the kingdom of God as it intrudes into the present order.

The Gospel readings:

We conclude our reading of the Gospel of John on Wednesday. The remainder of the gospel is read at other times in the two-year cycle. Our closing look at the gospel is the priestly prayer that Jesus offered at the Last Supper. First Jesus rememberd all that he had done in his life with the disciples. Then he offered his disciples to the Father: "Sanctify them in the truth..." (John 17:17a). The priest at the Eucharist remembers the mighty acts of God in history and in creation and then offers the bread and wine, saying, "Sanctify them by your Holy Spirit to be for your people the Body and Blood of your Son. . ." (BCP, p. 363)

We are to be a living sacrament of the Lord's presence in the world today. We are set apart, consecrated and sanctified, then sent forth into the world to live that sacramental presence. Note that the Lord prays for our unity. We must be seen by the world as the one Body of Christ or our witness will be diluted. We ". . .offer and present unto (God). . .our selves, our souls and bodies, to be a reasonable, holy and living sacrifice. . ." (BCP, p. 336).

On Thursday we begin reading the Gospel of Luke with the account of John the Baptist's ministry and Jesus' temptation.

The third week of Easter

The Old Testament readings:

The adventures of Daniel continue this week as we read chapters 3-6. Nebuchadnezzar has another frightening dream, and again Daniel comes to his rescue. This time the dream is more ominous; the king will go mad because of his sins against God. Nebuchadnezzar's only hope is to "break off your sins by practicing righteousness, and your iniquities by showing mercy to the oppressed, that there may perhaps be a lengthening of your tranquillity." (Daniel 4:27)

There is no historical record of Nebuchadnezzar's son, Belshazzar, who appears in Wednesday's reading. He is a literary figure created by the writer to add impact to the narrative. Belshazzar dares to use the sacred Temple vessels brought from Jerusalem at one of his great feasts. A strange hand suddenly appears and writes three mysterious words on the wall. The idiom, "the handwriting on the wall," comes from this well-known story. Again, Daniel is able to offer an interpretation to the king.

We end this week with another well-known story—Daniel in the lion's den. The message was clear to a Jewish people under persecution, tempted to compromise their faith in order to get along with the occupiers: Keep the faith, even to the point of breaking the laws of the state. Even in the face of martyrdom, the Lord will save you and, in the end, God's power will overcome the evil of the oppressor. In the time that this book was written, Jewish worship practices were punishable by death, so the story was especially poignant to a people who sometimes risked death even to offer simple prayers to God. This story follows a well-established pattern. The evil men who plotted Daniel's death are themselves killed by the same means they had chosen to eliminate Daniel. (See the Book of Esther, chapter 8.)

The message must be clear to the followers of Christ today. We, too, must have the courage to keep the faith in the face of those who would emasculate the church, either by attempting to secularize it or by persecuting it.

The Epistle readings:
We continue reading 1 John. Keeping the commandments of Christ is the only way of truly being a follower of Christ. We are to believe in the Gospel given to the church. Jesus is the Christ, the Son of God, and we must love in the way that he showed us in his life, suffering and death. Whoever keep these commandments "...abide in him, and he in them..." (1 John 3:24a) These words may sound familiar because they are paraphrased in the prayer of consecration: "...that he may dwell in us, and we in him." (BCP, p. 336)

Monday's reading sets forth a standard of faith, an orthodoxy. We must believe that "Jesus the Christ has come in the flesh." This orthodox statement would set the true follower of Christ apart from those who were coming into the church with heretical doctrines that denied that Christ was both man and Son of God.

On Tuesday we read a summary of the Gospel: "God is love, and he who abides in love abides in God, and God abides in him." (1 John 4:16) These words are soon followed by the warning: "If anyone says, 'I love God,' and hates his brother, he is a liar; for he who does not love his brother whom he has seen, cannot love God whom he has not seen." (1 John 4:20)

On Wednesday our reading opens with a simple statement of faith that circulated in the early church: "Jesus is the Christ." This creed must be on the lips of the Christian just as acts of love must shape the life of the Christian. This is the praxis statement of Christian faith, the putting into action of one's beliefs. We do our faith by the way we respond to God's people in justice and in acts of love and compassion.

Christ is synonymous with life, we learn on Wednesday, for Christ came to overcome the world through his baptism (the water) and his death (the blood). The letter ends with strong words of forgiveness for the sinner. Notice how similar the

113

closing words of this epistle are to the closing statements of the Gospel of John. Compare 1 John 5:13 with John 20:30-31.

Friday's and Saturday's readings come from the two very short epistles of 2 John and 3 John. These epistles were probably also written by the writer of 1 John. These letters are brief personal notes, sent with the same concern as 1 John. The church, the "Lady" in 2 John, must hold fast to the doctrine she was first taught. Third John deals with strife within the church presided over by the writer's friend, Gaius.

The Gospel readings:

From our beginning in the Gospel of Luke last week, we move more deeply into the body of that gospel this week. Luke was written for a gentile audience in about the year 85 A.D. It is one of the three synoptic gospels, meaning gospels written "through the same eye," or from the same perspective. Matthew, Mark, and Luke contain many of the same events and sayings of Jesus, though each one follows a different approach and is aimed at a different audience.

Luke's major concern in reporting the events of Jesus' life, death, and resurrection is to point out the universal nature of the Good News. Jesus has come so that all people, Jew and gentile alike, may know the salvation of God. It is not a salvation limited to one people or one time and place. Luke shows a particular concern for the poor and the oppressed. Watch for that concern as you read each day. For example, look at Luke 1:51-53: "He has shown strength with his arm, he has scattered the proud in the imagination of their hearts, he has put down the mighty from their thrones, and exalted those of low degree; he has filled the hungry with good things, and the rich he has sent empty away."

While Matthew talks about the poor in spirit being blessed (Mt. 5:3), Luke gives no such modification to the happiness of the poor in the sight of God: "Blessed are you poor, for yours is the kingdom of God." (Luke 6:20b) In Luke the rich who rely on their own strength and power are cursed: "But woe to you that are rich, for you have received your consolation." (Luke 6:24)

With the proclamation of the raising up of the poor and the oppressed and the bringing down of the powerful and rich, we have a very radical gospel at hand. These statements must be seen not just as statements of personal piety, but as prophetic utterances of political and social justice that come through the working of the Holy Spirit.

The writer of the Gospel of Luke points up the work of the Holy Spirit in ways that Matthew and Mark do not. It is the Holy Spirit that empowers the disciples of Jesus to carry on the ministry, to proclaim the coming of the kingdom, to heal, and to teach.

Through the reading of this gospel we also come to realize the extent of God's forgiveness for us who are sinners. The Parable of the Prodigal Son expresses the Gospel of forgiveness and restoration in a dramatic way.

Read Luke with the understanding that it is the first of a two-part work. Acts is the second half of Luke's Gospel, though separated in the New Testament by the Gospel of John. The Gospel of Luke gives us the universal message of salvation and healing as revealed through Jesus of Nazareth. In Acts, that salvation message is carried out by the church, empowered by the Holy Spirit. The apostles discover they have Christ's power of healing and proclamation for he dwells within them through the Holy Spirit. The church, the gathered followers of Jesus, goes out to the gentile world in the same way that Jesus had gone out to the Jews.

Watch for the themes of salvation, forgiveness, empowerment through the Holy Spirit, and the radical reordering of priorities in society as you read from the Gospel of Luke these coming days. Every word of this gospel has intense meaning for our own struggle in the world today.

In our readings this week we hear Jesus identify himself with the great words of the prophet, Isaiah:

> The Spirit of the Lord is upon me, because he has anointed me to preach good news to the poor. He has sent me to proclaim release to the captives and recovering sight to the blind, to set at liberty those who are oppressed, to proclaim the acceptable year of the Lord. (Luke 4:18-19)

These words, often quoted by those who espouse liberation theology, really set forth the nature of Jesus' words and actions among the people. No wonder Jesus threatened people from the very first. He threatened the established order of his time. He threatens the established order of our time, too. The downtrodden will be raised up by God and those who oppress God's poor and weak will inevitably be brought down by a God who works in history to restore, redeem, liberate and save.

The sudden shift of the people's mood from wonder to animosity came when Jesus indicated that their lack of faith in God's power kept that power from being shown in their midst. God had to show his presence outside Judah in earlier times, Jesus reminded them, and it was happening again in his life.

The fourth week of Easter

The Old Testament readings:

For the next two weeks we will be reading the Book of Wisdom found in the Apocrypha. This may have been the last book of the Apocrypha to have been written, dated about 50 B.C. Unlike most of the writings of the Old Testament that deal with the community's story of God's revelation to Israel, the wisdom literature is a distinct genre that deals with the concerns of the individual and the questions of personal struggle and fulfillment.

Why do the wicked prosper and the righteous folk of the world often seem to suffer? is one of the major questions of the the book. The Wisdom of Solomon was probably written by a Jew living in Egypt. His concern was not unlike the writer of Daniel. Jews living in Egypt faced an emerging literary, scientific, and philosophic world that tempted them away from their staid Jewish practices. The intellectual stimulation they were exposed to in Egypt made the faith of their ancestors pale by comparison. The writer of the Wisdom of Solomon reminded his readers that God is the ultimate source of wisdom. The quest for wisdom leads the follower into a close relationship with God, which gives man and woman an eternal destiny with God in contrast with the deadly end of the wicked.

God's presence is shown to man and woman in the personal touch of God's Spirit, here called wisdom. To seek wisdom is to draw close to God. Wisdom takes on a personality of its own: "...wisdom is a kindly spirit..." (Wisdom 1:6a) and again: "Wisdom is radiant and unfading, and she is easily discerned by those who love her..." (Wisdom 6:12) The biblical imagery of God includes female as well as male metaphors.

Monday's reading states the feelings of the wicked person. In Wisdom 2:9-11 we read:

Let none of us fail to share in our revelry, everywhere let us leave signs of enjoyment, because this is our portion, and this is our lot. Let us oppress the righteous poor man;

let us not spare the widow nor regard the gray hairs of
the aged. But let our might be our law of right, for what
is weak proves itself to be useless.

These words judge our value system in America today, as well
as those evident in first century Alexandria. The reading ends
with a reference to the imperishable nature that is available to
the righteous person in contrast to the spiritual death that leads
to the physical death of the unrighteous. These words nudge
us closer to an understanding of the resurrection proclaimed
in the gospels.

The strengthening word of immortality in God's presence become more profound with Tuesday's reading, which is one of
the options in the Book of Common Prayer for reading at a
burial. The souls of the righteous are with God, we read in
Wisdom 3:1-6.

But the souls of the righteous are in the hand of God,
and no torment will ever touch them. In the eyes of the
foolish they seem to have died, and their departure was
thought to be an affliction, and their going from us to be
their destruction; but they are at peace. For though in the
sight of men they were punished, their hope is full of immortality. Having been disciplined a little, they will receive
great good, because God tested them and found them
worthy of himself; like gold in the furnace he tried them,
and like a sacrificial burnt offering he accepted them.

The concept of divine judgment becomes the theme in Wednesday's reading. The time will come when the wicked who
have been scoffing at the suffering righteous will understand
the final outcome for themselves. They will die without a trace,
in contrast to the eternal reward of the righteous.

"She (wisdom) hastens to make herself known to those who
desire her. He who rises early to seek her will have no
difficulty." (Wisdom 6:13-14a) God reaches out to touch man
and woman in wisdom. This is one way that we are led closer
to God in the present moment and eternally. These words provide a seedbed for the Good News of the New Testament. Read

the prologue of John's Gospel, John 1:1-18. The Word, or Wisdom, was with God, ". . .and the Word was God," is the proclamation of Good News. Link those words with today's reading and you can trace the evolving understanding among the Jewish and Christian people of God's activity in the world. God reaches out to touch us through his Word. But the exciting reality in the New Testament, of course, is that this Wisdom took on flesh in the man, Jesus.

The Epistle readings:

Paul's letter to the Colossians is our focus this week and Monday of next week. How quickly our baptismal promises renewed at Easter can become distorted by the ideals and values of the society around us. Colossians, written by Paul to people he had never met, urged them back to the true Gospel and reminds us in Eastertide that we must be pulled back to the Gospel proclaimed in our baptism.

Prison was Paul's environment when he wrote this letter, either at Ephesus or Rome. Writing to virtual strangers, Paul must introduce himself. Their evangelist had been Paul's "beloved fellow servant," Epaphras. Though the church of Colossae had heard the true Gospel, they had soon succumbed to the impact of the religious understanding of their neighbors. It was not Christ who controlled nature and their destiny, they were told. Angels and mystical powers waged warfare against the believer. One must appease those angelic powers by elaborate ritual and constant seeking after the mysteries of the unseen powers. Thus, a whole level of intermediaries lay between a people and God, intermediaries who must be placated and satisfied. The Christianity revealed by Epaphras soon was replaced by a Christianity that promised the secret knowledge one needed to relate to the angelic powers.

This concern for angelic or heavenly cooperation is still an issue in our society today, with anxious glances at our horoscope and careful rituals perfomed to placate fate. It was against this false theology that Paul wrote so passionately from his prison confinement. Tuesday's reading is a beautiful creedal statement reminding the Christians of Colossae once again of the complete and utter pre-eminence of the risen Christ. There can be no intermediaries between the faithful and their risen Savior. It was into eternal relationship with this Christ that the Christians were baptized. The only mystery they need concern themselves with is the mystery of Christ, and that was a mystery revealed at baptism. In Christ, the Word of God became fully known: "...the mystery hidden for ages and generations but now made manifest to his saints." (Col. 1:26)

The theology of baptism is made clear in Thursday's reading: "...you were buried with him in baptism, in which you were also raised with him through faith in the working of God, who raised him from the dead." (Col. 2:12) Having been raised with Christ, let us keep our minds on Christ, Paul urged his readers.

The subject and feeling of the letter shifts in Friday's reading. Paul wrote about the practical applications of the faith to Christian life. Echoes of the well-known poem of love in 1 Corinthians 13 are heard in Saturday's text: "And above all these put on love, which binds everything together in perfect harmony." (Col. 3:14)

The Gospel readings:

Last Thursday we began reading Luke's counterpart to the Sermon on the Mount. This part of Luke is sometimes referred to as the Sermon on the Plain since Luke states that Jesus talked to the people on level ground. It was hard for Luke to know where and in what context Jesus made these statements. Placing the sayings together heightened their impact for the reader and hearer.

The fifth week of Easter

The Old Testament readings:

A poem of praise to wisdom, begun in Saturday's reading, is concluded in the Sunday lection. Wisdom is that attribute of God that ". . .pervades and penetrates all things." (Wisdom 7:24) Though the lectionary leaves out Wisdom 9:2-6 in Tuesday's reading, I'd suggest reading the passage. ". . .give me the wisdom that sits by thy throne. . ." Solomon prayed. (Wisdom 9:4a) The writer of the Wisdom of Solomon attributed those words to the great king who was known for his wisdom. The sense that wisdom was a divine personality of God reaching out to guide and touch man and woman is a strong message throughout the book. The theological understanding of the writer helped to lay the groundwork for understanding Christ who ". . .is seated at the right hand of the Father." (Nicene Creed). Christ is that attribute or personality of God that reaches out to man and woman to reveal to them the nature and will of God.

On Tuesday we begin a poetic treatment of Israel's early history. It was God's Wisdom who led Adam, Noah, Abraham, Lot, Jacob, Joseph, and Israelites, and Moses himself in the wilderness. Cain rejected Wisdom when he killed his brother. The people of Babel rejected Wisdom when they built their tower. It was Wisdom who confounded the Egyptians when they tried to block Israel's flight from Egypt.

Though pagans may worship nature, the beauty and wonder of nature should lead the faithful to see God's work in creation: "For from the greatness and beauty of created things comes a corresponding perception of their Creator." (Wisdom 13:5)

Another preview of Gospel revelation comes on Thursday when we read in Wisdom 15:3, ". . .to know thy power is the root of immortality." In the Gospel of John we read, "And this is eternal life, that they know thee the only true God, and Jesus Christ whom thou hast sent." (John 17:3) The writer of Wisdom was Jewish, not Christian, but his theological insights about the nature of God's wisdom helped prepare the way for the truth of God's presence that Jesus was to bring.

Friday's lection returns to the theme of God's wisdom acting in history. The reading contrasts the darkness of Egyptian life during the plagues with the blessings bestowed on the Israelites. "...so that thy sons, whom thou didst love, O Lord, might learn that it is not the production of crops that feeds man, but that thy word preserves those who trust in thee." (Wisdom 16:26) Jesus quoted similar words when he confronted Satan in the wilderness: "...It is written, 'Man shall not live by bread alone, but by every word that proceeds from the mouth of God.'" (Matt. 4:4)

The study of the Book of Wisdom ends as the week closes. The writer continues his poetic description of Israel's exodus from Egypt. Creation cooperated with God's will to save the people, even to the extent of the Red Sea drying up so that Israel could escape the Egyptians. The Lord plays upon the forces of nature the way a musician plays upon a lute.

The Epistle readings:

Paul concluded his letter to the Colossians with a list of greetings and with the mention of various people who were close to him in his ministry. Onesimus, mentioned in verse nine, was the runaway slave whom Paul wrote about in his letter to Philemon. Luke, the physician, mentioned in verse 14 was probably not the same Luke who wrote the Gospel according to Luke and the Book of Acts.

The optional portion of Monday's reading refers to family relationships. "Wives, be subject to your husbands, as is fitting in the Lord." (Col. 3:18) If we are going to quote that verse to support the idea of a patriarchal family system, we must also include Paul's admonitions a few verses on: "Slaves, obey in everything those who are your earthly masters...Whatever your task, work heartily, as serving the Lord and not men..." (Col. 3:22-23) Paul's words cannot be applied literally to social and ethical situations facing us today. He wrote to a particular people in a particular time. If we are to insist that wives be subject to their husbands as their duty to Christ, then we must take with equal weight Paul's admonition to slaves.

Our reading of the Epistle to the Romans was interrupted at the end of the fifth week of Lent with the special selections for Holy Week. We now conclude the reading of Romans as we turn to look at chapters 12 through 15 of the epistle. (Chapter 16 is composed mostly of personal greetings from Paul and is not included in our lectionary texts.)

"I appeal to you therefore, brethren, by the mercies of God, to present your bodies as a living sacrifice, holy and acceptable to God, which is your spiritual worship." (Romans 12:1). These beautiful words that greet us with Tuesday's reading find their echo in the familiar words of the eucharistic prayer from Rite 1: "And here we offer and present unto thee, O Lord, ourselves, our souls and bodies, to be a reasonable, holy and living sacrifice unto thee." (BCP, p. 336). What we offer at the Eucharist is not simply money, time or talent but our entire lives as a living sacrifice expressed in the symbols of what we have and who we are.

Wednesday's reading urges Christians to obey civil authority as civil authority represents the ultimate authority of God. This passage has been used to justify the Christian's blind obedience to government. But we must remember that Paul wrote out of his life experiences. The Roman government had protected him from the wrath of his own people. He wrote at a time when he hoped that the Christian church might somehow find legitimacy in the empire. He wrote as a citizen of that empire himself. Paul's words cannot be applied *carte blanche* to all situations and to all governments. Throughout the history of the church, Christians have found themselves standing against the government as a direct witness to the higher authority of God. Scripture provides many examples of this great witness, examples that dare not be neutralized by Paul's words of advice to the church in Rome.

Paul's major concern in the readings we share from Wednesday on is for Christian unity in the midst of diversity. One is not to judge the place another Christian is in. Some Christians will follow dietary laws that others do not, but what matters is their life in God and not their outward acts of devotion. A nonjudgmental stance must inform the life of the Christian community: "Welcome one another, therefore, as Christ has welcomed you, for the glory of God." (Romans 15:7). The New English Bible uses the word "accept" in place of the RSV translation "welcome." Within the diversity of life, Christians must speak out with one voice to the glory of God. (Romans 15:6) Paul's hope was that individuals would focus their actions not on themselves but on the good of the whole community, a community that looked beyond itself to the Christ who empowered it in the Holy Spirit.

An Advent theme is set in Wednesday's reading. We must wake up as out of a sleep for the time of Christ's deliverance is approaching. This text is appointed for reading at the Eucharist on the first Sunday in Advent, year A. The images of Advent are beautifully set forth in the text.

The Gospel readings:

This week we follow Jesus as he preaches, heals and forgives the repentant sinners of Galilee. As you read the assigned chapters, note how values, priorities and accepted situations in life are reversed with the words and actions of Jesus. The sick become well and even the dead are raised. A woman considered an outcast becomes the one sent off in peace, in contrast to the self-righteous dinner host. In an age when women were considered inferior to men, we find Jesus being accompanied by women as well as by men in his travels about Galilee. This was unheard of in Jesus' time. As the kingdom of God begins to be felt in the present age, the world is turned upside down. This, too, is Good News but it can be bad news for those who want to hold on to the old order and values. No wonder there was opposition to Jesus, to his followers, and to Paul. If the church today simply reflects the accepted standards, values and positions of the rest of society, we are not living close enough to the Gospel we read and espouse today.

The sixth week of Easter

The Old Testament readings:

The sixth week of the Easter season includes the important celebration of Ascension Day. According to the Book of Acts, Jesus appeared to his disciples for a period of 40 days. In one last appearance he promised them the Holy Spirit to empower them for ministry in his name and then ". . . he was lifted up, and a cloud took him out of their sight." (Acts 1:9b) From that time on the followers of Christ were guided, empowered, and inspired by the Holy Spirit, rather than by the risen Christ.

The Old Testament selections this week are chosen to help us sense the immediate power and presence of the Lord. We, too, are lifted up into the presence of the powerful God in our readings. Sunday's reading from the apocryphal Book of Ecclesiasticus provides a grand poem of praise for God's creative acts in the world around us. From surveying the wonder of God's presence in the natural world, the writer turned to poetic praise of this God who calls all creation into being.

On Monday and Tuesday, we turn to the Book of Deuteronomy and read the words attributed to Moses just before his death. He reviewed for the people all the wonders that God had done for them in the wilderness. When they entered the Promised Land, they were not to forget that it was the Lord's power that brought them there and not their own. They must continue to praise God in blessing and thanksgiving. Incidentally, parts of the readings for these two days are assigned for reading on Thanksgiving Day at the Eucharist.

Baruch, an apocryphal book ascribed to the secretary of Jeremiah the prophet, raised the question: "Who has gone up into heaven, and taken her (Wisdom), and brought her down from the clouds?" (3:29) Wisdom, in the Hebrew mind, was not simply human knowledge. Wisdom was that aspect of God that revealed the Lord's will for men and women. As the followers of Christ reflected on his life among them, they soon made the connection that in Christ Wisdom had, indeed, come down to man and woman in the flesh of a human being. That aspect of God known as Wisdom that reached out to communicate with people had now come into the world as Jesus, and the world would never be the same again.

Moreover, the Holy Spirit would be a continuing in-the-flesh experience of God's wisdom touching people, Christians discovered. However, the writer of Baruch was not referring to Christ as he wrote his powerful words of praise. He was a Jew who loved the Torah and felt that it was God's Wisdom fully revealed in the world.

On Ascension Day we begin a 10-day reading of the prophet Ezekiel. Ezekiel wrote during a traumatic time in our people's history. Jerusalem fell to the Babylonians in 587 B.C., and Judah's leading families were sent into exile in Babylonia. Ezekiel was one of the earlier exiles. Imagine the anguish of that moment, and the impression it made on the heartbroken refugees. Ever since the Israelites encountered the Lord at Mt. Sinai, they had been warned by Moses and the prophets who spoke in later generations that turning away from the demands of the covenant would result in disaster. Now this disaster was visited upon the nation as the people moved out of their homeland to go to an alien land.

Ezekiel wrote in visionary language, reflecting either ecstatic revelatory experiences that he had or a literary style that helped the reader reflect on the mystery of God's action in that awful time. The book receives a very cursory treatment in the daily lectionary. We read from Ezekiel during these 10 days and again for one week in proper one, year two.

As we concentrate this day on Jesus' ascension into the presence of God, it is appropriate to read Ezekiel's vision of the Lord's appearance to him as he stood on a riverbank in Babylonia following his exile from Judea. The vision described by Ezekiel is not easy to picture. Richard W. Anderson in his book, *Understanding the Old Testament,* describes the vision this way:

On looking further, he saw that the throne-chariot was borne by four weird creatures half animal and half

127

human...each moving in perfect coordination with the other because they were all animated by the divine Spirit. Alongside each cherub was a gleaming wheel—or rather, 'a wheel within a wheel' as though set at right angles to each other to enable the chariot to move easily in any direction, as the Spirit directed. And above the creatures was something like a crystal platform or firmament which was carried on the cherubs' wings with a roar like the sound of many waters. Looking still higher, the prophet saw above the firmament the likeness of a sapphire throne, and 'seated above the likeness of a throne was a likeness as it were of a human form.' In an ecstatic vision the prophet beheld Yahweh seated upon his lofty throne in dazzling radiance.*

As the Spirit entered into Ezekiel he found himself speaking to the Lord who handed the prophet a scroll and ordered him to eat it. The scroll tasted as sweet as honey. The Lord would place words in the prophet's mouth, words that would not be understood nor accepted by the Jewish people.

This vision of Ezekiel's call to be a prophet among the exiles echoes Isaiah's call when he was "lifted up" into the presence of the Lord and instructed to go and speak to a people who would not hear. Read Isaiah 6:1-13 and Jeremiah 1 to get a sense of the feelings associated with God's call to speak as a prophet. The language of vision and symbol is the only adequate medium to express the awesomeness of the call.

The Epistle readings:

We read from the Letter of James Monday through Wednesday. Scholars disagree over whether this letter was actually written by James, the brother of Jesus, or by a writer who lived later in the first century or early in the second century. The later dating seems more natural to me as I relate to the writing. James

---

*Richard W. Anderson, *Understanding the Old Testament* (Prentice-Hall, Inc., 1957) p. 364

writes for the church, giving guidance for Christian living. He has a strong sense of social justice for the poor. We are to be doers of the word, and not just hearers. Tuesday's reading is a confrontation to those who "listen and do not obey." Look at the definition of true religion in the closing verse of chapter 1.

On Ascension Day we again begin reading of Hebrews. As we think about Jesus ascending into heaven it is appropriate to think about the nature of Jesus as both Lord and Savior. Hebrews is appropriate to the task. The writer has just been speaking about the fragmentary ways the Lord has spoken to people in earlier times. Angels acted as mediators between God and mankind. But Jesus stands far above any angel. The writer quoted Psalm 8 to remind the reader that man and woman are "lower than the angels." Jesus became fully man, one who lived a life lower than the angels. If he was to deliver people from their bondage and lead them to glory, then he must fully identify with their human condition.

Melchizedek, the priest mentioned in Genesis 14:17-20 and in Psalm 110:4, is introduced in Friday's and Saturday's readings. We will meet him again in chapter 7 of Hebrews, and I'll talk more about him when we get to that chapter next week.

The Gospel readings:
The theme of suffering stated so passionately in Hebrews is reflected in the gospel reading for Monday. If one is to be a follower of Christ, one must take up the cross and follow the Lord. These words from Jesus may have been in the mind of the writer of Hebrews. On Tuesday we move ahead two chapters where we read Jesus' words about the need for persistence in prayer. The Lord's Prayer helps us keep our thoughts and actions on the coming kingdom of God, a kingdom that Christ came to proclaim in his life, death, resurrection and ascension. The need to keep one's mind on the kingdom, rather than on the riches and temptations of the present time is the theme expressed again in Wednesday's reading. Don't be anxious about the everyday things of your life, Jesus urged. Look at the lilies of the field and the birds of the air, see how God clothes

the lilies in beauty and feeds the birds what they need. "But seek first his kingdom and his righteousness, and all these things shall be yours as well." (Matt. 6:33)

Thursday is Ascension Day, and our lection is Jesus' great commission to go forth and baptize in the name of the Trinity. Jesus, the man who lived as one of us, was more than man. He pointed with his life to a reality that exists beyond time, space and temporal creation, and yet a reality that touches every aspect of our lives. The ascension of Jesus is as much a theological statement as a moment in history. Jesus the man was lifted up. His being lifted up raises our life to a new significance as well. We, too, live in this world and yet our lives point beyond the present struggle to the realm of God made known to us through the same Jesus who came and lived among us. The gospel is not read in sequence this week as it is for most weeks of the year. As we approach the major feast of Ascension Day our thoughts are directed toward the realm of God, a realm lived out by Jesus and proclaimed accessible to us in the celebration.

On Friday and Saturday we return to the sequential reading of the Gospel of Luke, with the story of Jesus' transfiguration and the frustration he immediately experienced as he came down from the mount.

The seventh week of Easter
Year One

The Old Testament readings:

In the year 598 B.C. the Babylonians invaded Judah and deported the leading citizens of the nation. They sent King Jehoiakim off into exile leaving his uncle, Zedekiah, in Jerusalem as a puppet ruler for the people. Ezekiel began his prophetic speaking among the Babylonian exiles in 593, five years after the initial invasion. Last week we read the description of Ezekiel's ecstatic trance in which he felt the call to be a prophet before the exiles. As we begin this week in the Book of Ezekiel we hear further words of commissioning felt by the prophet. He must speak out to warn the people as a watchman speaks out to warn a doomed city. Not to speak warning is to accept the responsibility for the people's sins. Ezekiel's understanding of the Lord's will for him and the people is expressed in symbolic and poetic language to add impact to his words.

The exiles in Babylonia lived with the hope that Jehoiakim would be restored on the throne in Jerusalem so that their defeat and captivity would be short-lived. The Babylonians had captured the city, but left it intact. Judah still had a king in Jerusalem, Zedekiah, though he acted under the authority of the Babylonians. Surely God would act in their favor soon. Against these false hopes, Ezekiel spoke out with brutal truth. The visions read on Monday describe the ultimate destruction of Jerusalem that Ezekiel foresaw. In his vision he was ordered to lie first on one side and then on the other, an ominous sign of Israel's extended exile. The people back home would eat rationed food. They would be forced to break their dietary rituals in the face of further siege and destruction. More words of doom are read on Tuesday. The economy of Judah will be in utter ruin as the nation finally falls before the onslaught of the enemy.

In 589 the puppet king, Zedekiah, attempted to revolt against the Babylonians. Again the Babylonian armies swept into the land. After a siege, the city fell. This time the Temple and much of the city were destroyed. The visions of Ezekiel now became a reality. The prophet kept in close touch with his homeland during his time of exile. He heard of the false hope, the rumors of rebellion, and the final destruction of his beloved city. New refugees arrived from Judah during those awful years. The city finally fell in 587, but deportations continued until 581. All of the leading families of Judah found themselves living in an alien land. Once the city had been destroyed, Ezekiel turned from words of doom and lament to words of hope. A new day was coming, he proclaimed. Now Judah could turn her attention to restoration in the light of the Lord's blessing.

Words of hope greet us on Wednesday. Israel will experience a new exodus, one at least as glorious as the exodus from Egypt so many years before. The Lord will give the people a new heart and a new spirit, and the Lord will truly become the people's God once more. Though it may sound as though Ezekiel had been in Judah during the final days of destruction, chances are that he had been in Babylonia all along. Reports from the homeland were frequent. His ecstatic visions added to his sense of immediacy when he spoke of Jerusalem.

The sins of the parents would be visited upon the children. The sins of one's past could never be completely forgiven. These were the understandings of the people at the time of Ezekiel. Not so, said the prophet; each person stands individually responsible. The words of Ezekiel read on Thursday provided a tremendous movement in theological understanding for the Jews.

The Lord as shepherd of the people is a familiar motif in both the Hebrew Scriptures and in the gospels. The shepherd theme is beautifully expressed by Ezekiel in the text assigned for Friday. Social justice is demanded by the prophet. "Is it not enough for you to feed on the good pasture, that you must tread down with your feet the rest of your pasture, and to drink of clear water, that you must foul the rest with your feet?" (Ezek.

34:18) In one's greed for wealth and power, one must not trample on the rights of another. Such "rams and he-goats" will be judged, the prophet warned. The mention of the Lord's servant, David, expresses the hope of a righteous king once again sitting as king of the people, a king who will be a descendant of David.

As we leave Ezekiel on Saturday, we read of the Lord's glory again filling the Temple. That holy place will no longer be overshadowed by the king's palace and the bones of dead nobility. The Temple shall stand separate as the dwelling place of the mighty God. Ezekiel is read for one additional week in year 2. At that time other well-known sections of the prophet's writings are shared, including the vision of the dry bones.

The Epistle readings:

Strong words of warning that had a deep influence on the primitive church launch this week in Hebrews. One who accepts Christ and then falls away from the faith cannot hope to be restored. It's as if they have crucified Christ all over again. These words were taken literally by the church in some cases. "Keep the faith," was the writer's command, even in the face of the worst persecution.

Melchizedek was introduced last week in chapter 5. A brief reference to this person is found in Genesis 14:17-20 and again in Psalm 110:4. The writer of Hebrews uses that brief reference to lay a groundwork for understanding Jesus' role as great high priest. Melchizedek must represent a higher order of priests than the Levites, a priest forever, according to Psalm 110. The "for ever" nature of this strange priest stemmed partly from the fact that Genesis does not mention Melchizedek's family ties. Consequently, the writer of Hebrews assumed that he must have been one who lived beyond the pale of history and of time. It is this order of Melchizedek that lays the groundwork for understanding Jesus' role as great high priest.

Unlike the priests of the Temple, Jesus does not need to make continual sacrifices year after year, for Jesus made a perfect sacrifice once and for all. "Consequently, he is able for all time to save those who draw near to God through him, since he always lives to make intercession for them." (Heb. 7:25) The writer of Hebrews understood life in this world as a mere shadow, or foretaste, of the perfect life in the world to come. The old covenant made with Moses on the mountain was an imperfect covenant. The prophets of old had known that. Jeremiah spoke of the new covenant written on the hearts of the people.

Saturday's reading continues the comparison of the imperfect sacrifices of the Temple priests with the perfect sacrifice of Christ. We get a good description of Temple worship in Jesus' time as ritual practices are outlined.

We end our reading of Hebrews without finishing the book. It is read again in year 2 during the season of Epiphany.

The Gospel readings:

The mood of the Gospel of Luke changes this week as we move into another major section of the work. "Jesus set his face to go to Jerusalem," we read on Monday. He prepared himself and his disciples for what he knew would happen there as he came face to face with the opposition of the established authorities. Read the assigned passages with a sense of dread of what was to come. When Jesus spoke of the hardships of being an apostle, he felt the shadow of the cross even as he talked.